Study Guide for
TECHNICAL ANALYSIS OF THE FUTURES MARKETS
A Self-Training Manual

ABOUT THE PUBLISHER
The New York Institute of Finance . . .
. . . more than just books.

NYIF offers practical, applied education and training in a wide range of financial topics:

* *Classroom training:* evenings, mornings, noon-hour
* *Seminars:* one- and two-day professional and introductory programs
* *Customized training:* need-specific, on your site or ours, in New York City, throughout the United States, anywhere in the world
* *Independent study:* self-paced learning—basic, intermediate, advanced
* *Exam preparation:* NASD licensing (including Series 7), CFA prep, state life and health insurance licensing

Subjects of books and training programs include the following:

* *Account Executive Training*
* *Brokerage Operations*
* *Futures Trading*
* *International Corporate Finance*
* *Options as a Strategic Investment*
* *Securities Transfer*
* *Technical Analysis*

When Wall Street professionals think **training**, they think **NYIF**.

Please write or call for our catalog:

New York Institute of Finance
70 Pine Street
New York, NY 10270–0003
212 / 344–2900

Simon & Schuster, Inc.   A Gulf + Western Company
"Where Wall Street Goes to School" ™

Study Guide for TECHNICAL ANALYSIS OF THE FUTURES MARKETS

A Self-Training Manual

John J. Murphy

New York Institute of Finance
Prentice-Hall

Library of Congress Cataloging-in-Publication Data

Murphy, John J.
  A study guide for Technical analysis of the futures markets.

  Designed to be used exclusively with the author's Technical analysis of the futures markets.
    1. Commodity exchanges. I. Murphy, John J. Technical analysis of the futures market. II. Title.
HG6046.M87 1986 Suppl.   332.64′4   87-10991
ISBN 0-13-858747-7

This publication is designed to provide accurate and authoritative information in regard to the subject matter covered. It is sold with the understanding that the publisher is not engaged in rendering legal, accounting, or other professional service. If legal advice or other expert assistance is required, the services of a competent professional person should be sought.

From a Declaration of Principles Jointly Adopted by a Committee of the American Bar Association and a Committee of Publishers and Associations

© 1987 by NYIF Corp.
  A Division of Simon & Schuster, Inc.
  70 Pine Street, New York, NY 10270-0003

All rights reserved. No part of this book may be reproduced in any form or by any means without permission in writing from the publisher.

Printed in the United States of America

10 9 8 7 6 5 4 3 2 1

New York Institute of Finance
(NYIF Corp.)
70 Pine Street
New York, NY 10270-0003

Contents

How to Use This Workbook, ix

LESSON ONE
**Technical Analysis
and the Dow Theory,** 1

LESSON TWO
Chart Construction, 7

LESSON THREE
Basic Concepts of Trend, 13

LESSON FOUR
**Major Reversal Patterns
and Continuation Patterns,** 25

LESSON FIVE
Volume and Open Interest, 35

LESSON SIX
**Long-Term Charts
and Commodity Indices,** 45

Midterm Examinations, 48

LESSON SEVEN
Moving Averages, 65

LESSON EIGHT
**Oscillators
and Contrary Opinion, 77**

LESSON NINE
**Point and
Figure Charting, 89**

Final Examination, 103

How to Use This Workbook

This self-study manual has been designed and prepared by the New York Institute of Finance, with the cooperation and input of John J. Murphy.

This workbook is to be used exclusively with John J. Murphy's *Technical Analysis of the Futures Markets* (referred to as the "text").

The workbook's objective is to test—and thereby to ensure—your comprehension of the large body of knowledge associated with technical analysis.

The methodology is simple to follow and uses your time efficiently. Here are the recommended steps:

• Before reading the textbook, go to Lesson One in the *Manual* (page 1). There you will find the Reading Assignment, which for the first lesson is Chapters 1 and 2 of the text. You will also find a set of reading Objectives and a Reading Orientation, which give your reading focus and direction. Also note the list of Key Terms (page 2). Following each term is a page reference, indicating where in the text you can find a definition or explanation of the term. Pay special attention to these terms.

- Then read the chapters assigned for the lesson. As you read, stay aware of the objectives and key terms. Ask questions of the text. Don't be afraid to underline what you feel is important—or make marginal notes.
- Then go to the Challenge section of the lesson (starting on page 3). There you will find a Matching Quiz, Multiple Choice, and sometimes Fill-In questions. Answer the questions "closed book" as best you can.
- Next turn to the Answer Sheet, and compare your answers against those given there. To "grade" yourself on these exams, divide the number of correct answers by the total number of answers and multiply the answer by 100. The result is your percentage right. Should your "grade" be lower than 65%, we suggest your re-reading the material for that lesson.

The purpose of this comparison, however, is *not* to give yourself a grade. Rather, it is to determine the areas where your comprehension is weak. Toward that end, each answer has a page reference to the text and a brief explanation of why the answer is correct. We suggest that you follow up these page references by re-reading the relevant sections of the text and making sure you understand the answer.

Once you have taken these steps for Chapters 1 and 2, proceed with Lesson Two, beginning on page 7.

This workbook has been class-tested at the New York Institute of Finance and produced with the utmost concern for accuracy and freedom from error. Nevertheless, we welcome your comments with regard to improvement. Please feel free to send your suggestions and observations to:

New York Institute of Finance
Publishing Division
70 Pine Street
New York, NY 10270-0003

Study Guide for TECHNICAL ANALYSIS OF THE FUTURES MARKETS

A Self-Training Manual

LESSON ONE

Technical Analysis and the Dow Theory

READING ASSIGNMENT

Chapters 1 and 2 of the text.

OBJECTIVES

- Understand the basic terms, concepts, and premises of technical analysis.
- Distinguish fundamental from technical analysis.
- Distinguish the Random Walk and Dow Theories.

READING ORIENTATION

Chapters 1 and 2 deal largely with the basis and background of technical analysis. As you progress in the course, you will see again and again the terms and concepts that are introduced in these chapters. For now, a general understanding of the basic terms is adequate.

Before reading the assignment, review the key terms on the next page. Look for them as you read. When you've completed your reading, go to page 3.

KEY TERMS

accumulation, 27
chartist, 12–13
confirmation, 27–28
correction, 26
day trading, 8
descriptive statistics, 19–20
distribution, 27
divergence, 27
Dow Theory
efficient market hypothesis, 20–21
failure swing, 31
flow of funds analysis, 16
fundamentalist approach, 5–6
inductive statistics, 19–20
market action, 1–2
price action, 1–2
technician, 12–13
trends, 26, 27, 30
trend trading, 8
volume, 28–29

Challenge

MATCHING QUIZ

Match each term at the left with a definition at the right, by placing the number of the definition in the fill-in space next to the term. A definition may be used more than once. There are more definitions than terms. The first term has been matched for you.

__8__ accumulation
__17__ chartist
__7__ confirmation
__2__ correction
__3__ day trading
__12__ descriptive statistics
__10__ distribution
__1__ divergence
__20__ Dow Theory
__11__ efficient market hypothesis
__2__ failure swing
__13__ flow of funds analysis
__6__ fundamentalist approach
__16__ inductive statistics
__5__ market action
__5__ raw data for chartist
__11__ Random Walk Theory
__18__ technical analysis
__21__ technician
__15__ trend
__14__ trend trading
__9__ volume

1. Either the Industrial or the Rail average gives the signal, not both.
2. Usually retraces 33% to 50%.
3. Trading intra-day changes, tic by tic.
4. The market has these trends.
5. Price, volume, open interest.
6. Study of the effect of supply and demand on commodity prices.
7. The Industrial and Rail averages give the signal.
8. Informed buying by astute investors.
9. A secondary indicator that should expand in the direction of the trend.
10. Informed selling.
11. Price behavior is "serially independent" and unpredictable.
12. Presentation of data.
13. Study of cash positions.
14. Intermediate term trading.
15. A pattern of successively rising or dropping peaks and troughs.
16. Generalizing, projecting, and predicting on the basis of collected data.
17. One who makes subjective judgments in analyzing market action.
18. Study of market action through charting, in order to forecast future trends.
19. The pricing structure of commodities.
20. Market action discounts everything.
21. Makes use of computers to analyze price behavior.

MULTIPLE CHOICE

Circle the letter of the correct answer. The first question is answered for you.

1. Which of the following is *not* a premise of technical analysis?
    a. History is repetitive.
    (b.) Price action reflects market action.
    c. Prices move in trends.
    d. Any influence on market action is reflected in prices.

2. Which of the following is *not* true of the fundamentalist's approach to analysis?
    a. The technical approach includes the fundamental method.
    b. Market prices tend to lead fundamental indicators.
    c. Fundamental analysis studies supply and demand.
    (d.) Fundamental analysis studies market action.

3. In which way is technical analysis the same or similar in both futures and stocks?
    a. Pricing structure.
    b. Margin requirements.
    c. Timing.
    (d.) None of the above.

4. Which statement best describes the Random Walk Theory?
    a. Past price movements are indicators of future movements.
    (b.) Price changes cannot be predicted.
    c. You can beat the market by buying many stocks at random.
    d. Market prices discount everything.

5. Which statement best describes the Dow Theory?
    a. Price changes may be used as indicators of future market action.
    b. Each stock must be considered separately from trends in the averages.
    (c.) Averages discount everything.
    d. None of the above.

6. The average length of a minor trend is:
    (a.) Less than 3 weeks.
    b. A month or more.
    c. About 3 months.
    d. Under 6 months.

7. Which of the following is a Dow Theory premise?

   a. The market has four trends: up, down, sideways, and regressive.

   b. Averages need not confirm one another.

   c. Market action discounts everything.

   d. Reversals must be expected at any time, unless a trend gives definite signals of remaining in effect.

8. Which statement is not true of any trend, according to Dow Theory?

   a. It may consist of primary, intermediate, and near-term categories of price movement.

   b. It consists of three phases.

   c. It should be confirmed by volume.

   d. A trend is likely to reverse itself at any time.

9. Which are criticisms of the Dow Theory?

   I. You cannot buy or sell the Dow averages.

   II. Volume is not included in the analysis.

   III. Its signals are too late.

   a. I only.

   b. I and II only.

   c. I and III only.

   d. I, II, and III.

10. In the following chart, which point(s) is (are) best described as a buy signal?

   I. A, C, and E.

   II. B1 and B2.

   III. D.

   a. I only.

   b. II only.

   c. II and III only.

   d. III only.

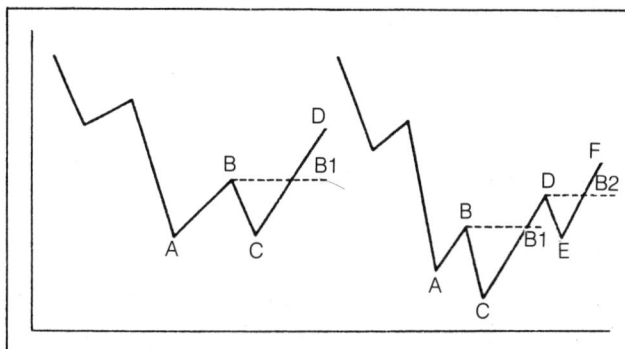

LESSON ONE

Answer Sheet

MATCHING QUIZ

8	1	5
17	20	5
7	11	11
2	2	18
3	13	21
12	6	15
10	16	14
		9

MULTIPLE CHOICE

1. b See pages 2–4 of the text.

2. d Fundamental analysis focuses on supply and demand underlying market action. See page 5.

3. d See pages 6–7. More specifically, see pages 13–17.

4. b To see why answer b is rejected by technical analysts, see page 21.

5. c See page 27.

6. a See page 26.

7. c Answer a cannot be correct because Dow recognized only three trends (see p. 26). Answer b is not correct (see p. 27). Pages 30–31 explain why answer d is not true.

8. d See pages 26–29 to see why answers a, b, and c are wrong. Pages 30–31 explain why answer d is not true.

9. c For proof of answer I, see the top of page 33. For evidence of answer III, see the bottom of page 32.

10. b See page 31.

LESSON TWO

Chart Construction

READING ASSIGNMENT

Chapter 3 of the text.

OBJECTIVES

- Identify bar, line, and point and figure charts.
- Read the information and identify the elements contained in a bar chart.
- Distinguish volume from open interest.
- Read the "Future Prices" in the financial news.

READING ORIENTATION

For some, this lesson may seem basic. If you have already achieved the objectives of this lesson, you might overlook reading Chapter 3 in the text, but take the quizzes in this lesson.

KEY TERMS

daily bar chart, 36
intra-day bar chart, 48
line chart, 36
open interest, 44
point and figure chart, 37
volume, 43

Challenge

MATCHING QUIZ

__2__ daily bar chart
__7__ intra-day bar chart
__5__ line chart
__1__ open interest
__3__ point and figure chart
__6__ volume

1. All outstanding contracts at end of trading.
2. Presents day-to-day price action data by means of vertical rules in series.
3. Presents price action data by means of x's and o's.
4. Presents market action data in terms of volume only.
5. Presents market action data by means of straight lines connecting plotted points.
6. All contracts traded during the day.
7. Presents price action for a period of less than one day.

MULTIPLE CHOICE

1. Which chart is used the most in futures technical analysis?
   a. Point and figure.
   b. Line chart.
   c. Intra-day chart.
   (d.) Daily bar chart.

Refer to the following charts for questions 2–5:

a.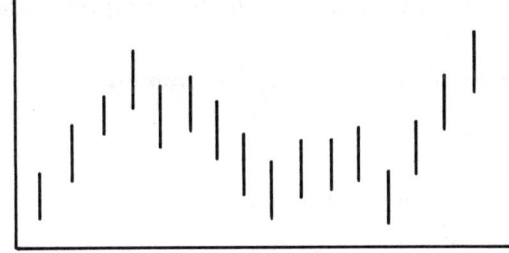

b.

c.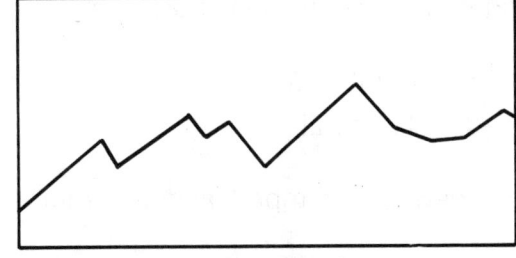

d.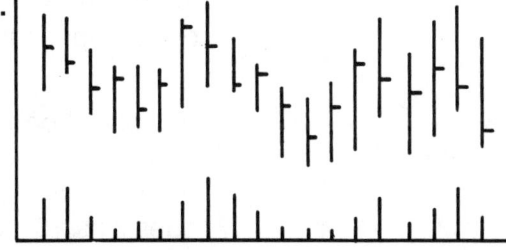

LESSON TWO

2. Which is a point and figure chart? *b*
3. Which is a bar chart? *a*
4. Which is a line chart? *c*
5. Which reflects volume? *d*
6. The horizontal tic to the right of a bar represents the:
    a. Average price for the day.
    (b.) Closing price.
    c. Opening price.
    d. Cumulative average price.
7. Which statement best defines *volume*?
    a. The total number of outstanding contracts held by market participants at the close.
    (b.) The total amount of trading activity in that commodity for the day.
    c. The total amount of trading activity in the commodities market in general.
    d. The total amount of trading activity as reflected in the Commodity Research Bureau Index.
8. Which statement best defines *open interest*?
    (a.) The total number of outstanding contracts held by market participants at the close.
    b. The total amount of trading activity in that commodity for the day.
    c. The total amount of trading activity in the commodities market in general.
    d. The total amount of trading activity as reflected in the Commodity Research Bureau Index.
9. Which statements are *true*?
    I. High open interest reflects high liquidity.
    II. High open interest reflects heavy trading.
    III. Buying and selling on high open interest are easier than on low open interest.
    a. I only.
    b. I and II only.
    (c.) I and III only.
    d. I, II, and III.

Refer to the following newspaper report and diagram for questions 10–15:

	Open	High	Low	Settle	Change	Lifetime High	Lifetime Low	Open Interest
Crude oil, Light Sweet (NYM) 42,000 gal., $ per bbl.								
Jan	26.70	26.84	26.47	26.80	+.04	31.50	26.45	5,112
Feb	26.73	26.81	26.46	26.78	+.01	31.30	26.47	23,212
Mar	26.57	26.71	26.38	26.70	.....	31.45	26.37	16,343

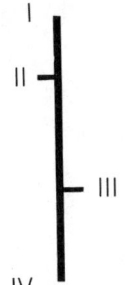

10. For February crude oil, point I on the bar chart would be:
   a. 26.73
   b. 26.81
   c. 26.46
   d. 26.78

11. For January crude oil, point II would be:
   a. 26.70
   b. 26.47
   c. 26.80
   d. 31.50

12. For January crude oil, point III would be:
   a. 26.70
   b. 26.47
   c. 26.80
   d. 31.50

13. For March crude oil, point IV is:
   a. 26.38
   b. 26.70
   c. 31.45
   d. 26.37

14. The previous day's closing price for January crude oil was:
   a. 26.76
   b. 26.80
   c. 26.84
   d. Cannot be determined.

15. Which month has the greatest total number of outstanding contracts at the end of the day?
   a. January
   b. February
   c. March
   d. Cannot be determined.

LESSON TWO

Answer Sheet

MATCHING QUIZ

        2   1
        7   3
        5   6

MULTIPLE CHOICE

1. d Despite the fact that other types of charts are used (point and figure or longer-term bar charts), the daily bar chart is by far the most commonly employed (see bottom of p. 35, top of p. 36).

2. b Compare this chart with the one on page 39 of the text or Figure 11.2 on page 326.

3. a or d Compare either chart with Figure 3.4 (p. 38) or Figure 3.7 (p. 41).

4. c Compare this chart with Figure 3.2 (p. 37).

5. d The vertical bars at the base of the chart reflect volume (see p. 43).

6. b See page 41.

7. b Answer a is open interest (p. 44). Answer c is not correct because, on a chart, volume refers to trading in the contract being charted, not in the commodities market as a whole. Alternative d is out; volume on a chart has nothing to do with the CRB index.

8. a This definition comes right off the first paragraph of page 44. Answers b, c, and d have already been eliminated in the explanation for question 7.

9. c Alternative I is true, as explained at the bottom of page 45. The second alternative is not necessarily true, since the number of outstanding contracts can remain high from one day to the next without heavy trading. For alternative III, again see the bottom of page 45.

10. b Point I is the high for the day—that price is in the second column over from "Feb."

11. a Point II (the tic to the left of the bar) is the opening price for the day—the first price after "Jan."

12. c Point III (the tic to the right of the bar) is the closing price for the day—the number under the heading "Settle."

13. a Point IV is the intra-day low. You'll find that number under the heading "Low."

14. a This number is not on the chart as such. To arrive at it, deduct the changes of +.04 from the present day's settle price: 26.80 less .04 equals 26.76. You deduct the +.04 because the change from yesterday was upward. If the number were negative, such as −.04, the change from yesterday would be negative; so you add the −.04.

15. b By definition, the "greatest total number of outstanding contracts" is open interest. If you look at the "Open Interest" figures for these contracts (last column), you see that the February contract has the highest open interest.

LESSON THREE

Basic Concepts of Trend

READING ASSIGNMENT

    Chapter 4 of the text.

OBJECTIVES

- Identify the directions and classifications of trends.
- Recognize support, resistance, and significant penetration.
- Understand the meaning of a channel line.
- Perceive and interpret retracement and speedlines.
- Identify reversal days and gaps in price action.

READING ORIENTATION

    The challenge section in this lesson is geared to test not only your understanding of, but also your ability to apply, the concepts in these chapters. While making up your own charts is neither suggested nor required, you will be asked to interpret patterns in several charts.

KEY TERMS

breakaway gap, 98
climax, 95
common gap, 98
correction, 56–58
downtrend, 54
exhaustion gap, 101
intermediate trend, 56
island reversal, 101–102
key reversal day, 95–96
major trend, 56
measuring gap, 100
near-term trend, 56
outside day, 95
resistance, 58, 76
retracement, 88–89
reversal, 60
reversal day, 94–95
sideways trend, 55
speedlines, 91
support, 58, 76
time filter, 74
trading range, 55
trendless, 55, 71
trendlines, 68
uptrend, 54

Challenge

MATCHING QUIZ

__21__ breakaway gap
__3__ climax
__18__ common gap
__6__ correction
__1__ downtrend
__13__ intermediate trend
__11__ island reversal
__17__ key reversal day *
__4__ major trend
__12__ measuring gap
__19__ near term trend
__14__ outside day
__15__ resistance
__6__ retracement
__16__ reversal *
__20__ reversal day *
__2__ sideways trend
__9__ speedline
__7__ support
__5__ time filter
__2__ trading range
__2__ trendless
__9__ trendlines
__8__ uptrend

1. A pattern of descending peaks and troughs.
2. A flat, horizontal pattern.
3. Bottom reversal day.
4. Longer than a year.
5. Successive closes beyond the trendline.
6. Price action that is not in the trend's direction but that does not affect the direction of the trend itself.
7. Price cannot go below this level.
8. A pattern of ascending peaks and troughs.
9. Measures the angle of a trend.
10. Period during which investors stay out of the market.
11. Reversal pattern with gaps before and after it.
12. Gap used to estimate the distance of a trend.
13. Three weeks to a few months.
14. Both the high and low on reversal day exceed those of the day before.
15. Prices cannot rise above this level.
16. Change in a trend's direction.
17. Identifiable only after significant movement of prices in opposite direction.
18. Shows a lack of trading interest in a thin market.
19. Two or three weeks.
20. Prices set a new extreme in the trend's direction during trading, but close in the opposite direction.
21. Gap that signals a significant market move.
22. An intra-day chart.
23. In an uptrend, a bearish gap.

LESSON THREE

MULTIPLE CHOICE

Refer to the following charts to answer questions 1–7:

a.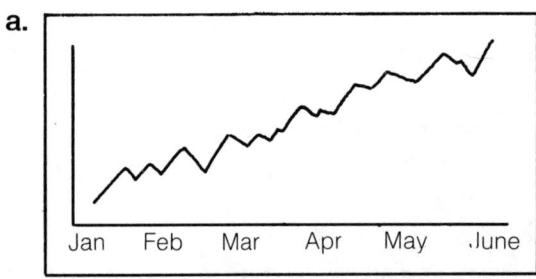

b.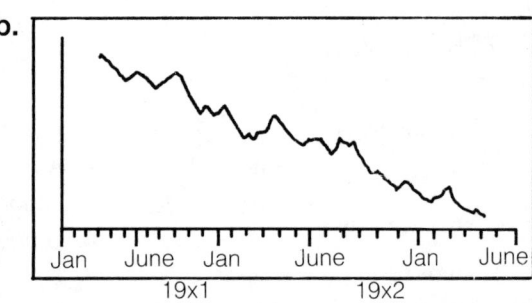

c.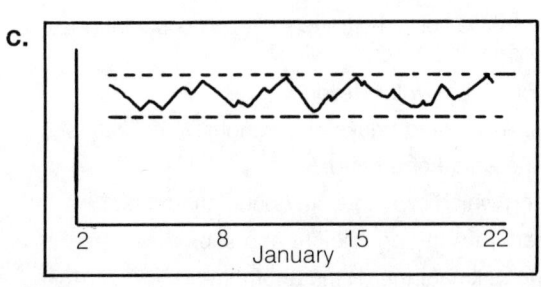

d.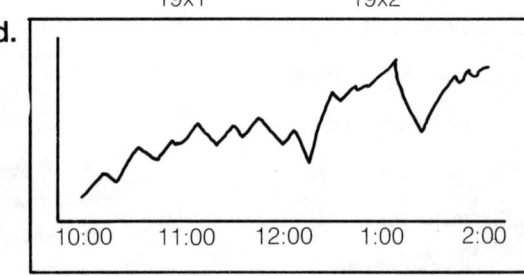

1. Which chart displays a sideways trend? c
2. Which chart shows an up trend? a, d
3. Which chart is trendless? c
4. In chart c, what do you call the area between the dashed lines?
    a. Support zone.
    b. Resistance area.
    (c.) Trading range.
    d. Retracement range.
5. Which chart shows intra-day trading? d
6. Which chart shows a situation indicating that staying out of the market is best? c
7. At a support level:
    (a.) Buying pressure overcomes selling pressure.
    b. Selling pressure overcomes buying pressure.
    c. Buying and selling pressures stay equal.
    d. Prices turn downward.

8. Select the truest statement about resistance:
   a. It is a price level over the market.
   b. Buying pressure overcomes selling pressure.
   c. It cannot be penetrated.
   d. The chartest sets its level.

Refer to the following chart to answer questions 9–12:

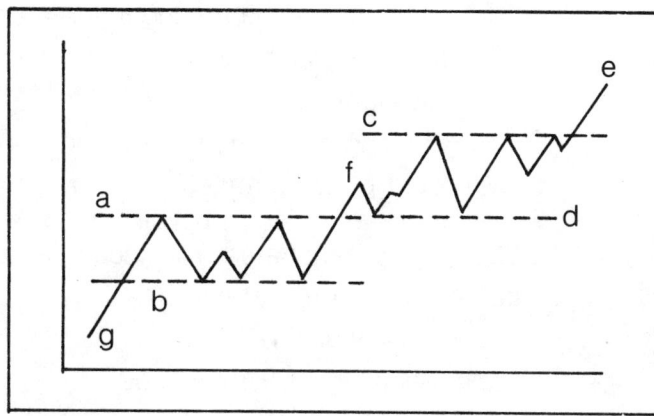

9. Which dashed lines represent support levels?
   a. a and c.
   b. b and d.
   c. a and b.
   d. c and d.
10. The principle shown by dashed line a–d is best described as:
    a. Continuous
    b. Corrective
    c. Role reversal
    d. Retracement
11. Which of the following does the chart *not* show?
    a. Support and resistance in an uptrend.
    b. Support and resistance in a downtrend.
    c. Trading ranges in an uptrend.
    d. A distinct uptrend.

12. Which solid lines clearly represent penetrations of resistance?
   a. e only.
   b. e and f only.
   c. e, f, and g only.
   d. None of the above.

13. Which is not a question to ask to gauge the significance of either support or resistance?
   a. How recent is the trading in the area?
   b. How heavy is the volume?
   c. How high is the open interest?
   d. How long have prices traded in this area?

14. With gold prices threatening to drop below $300 an ounce, you want to prevent a loss, but you wish to sell only in the event that the $300 level is penetrated. You should place a sell stop order at:
   a. A price slightly above $300.
   b. Precisely at $300.
   c. A price slightly below $300.
   d. A sell stop order is inappropriate for this purpose.

Refer to the following charts to answer questions 15–16:

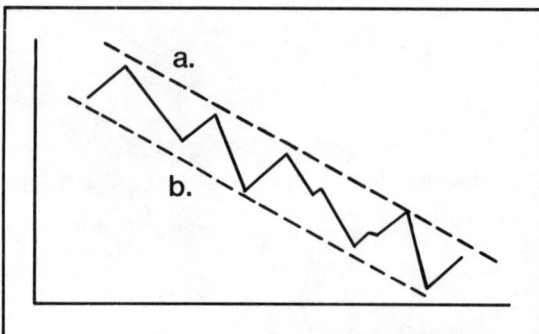 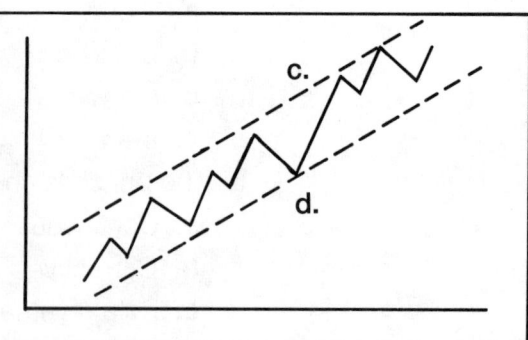

15. Which dashed line represents an uptrend line?
16. Which dashed line represents a downtrend line?

Refer to the following chart to answer questions 17–19:

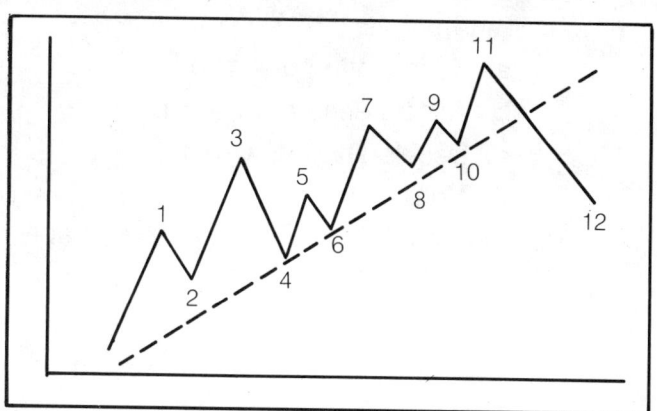

17. Which points in the trend may be used as buying areas?
   a. 1, 3, 5, 7, 9, 11
   b. 6, 8, 10
   c. 2, 4, 6, 8, 10, 12
   d. 5, 6, 7, 8, 9, 10

18. Which line(s) signal(s) a downside trend reversal?
   a. 4, 6, 10, 12
   b. 5, 9
   c. 12
   d. None.

19. Which is the least significant indicator of a trend reversal?
   a. A penetration of the trendline of more than 3%.
   b. A penetration two days in a row.
   c. A closing price beyond the trendline.
   d. An intra-day penetration.

Refer to the following chart to answer questions 20–25:

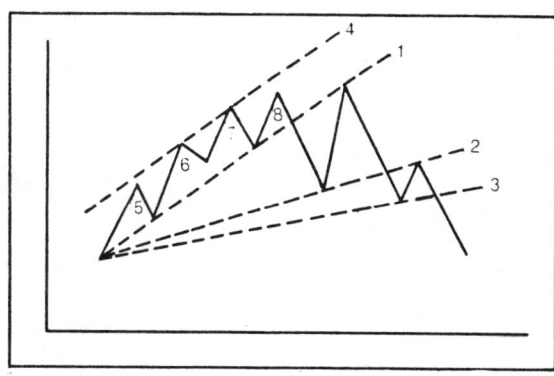

LESSON THREE

21

20. The trend is:
   a. Accelerating upward.
   b. Accelerating downward.
   c. Decelerating downward.
   d. None of the above.

21. The penetration of which line probably represents a trend reversal?
   a. 1
   b. 2
   c. 3
   d. 4

22. The chart is an example of:
   a. Head and shoulders.
   b. Fan principle.
   c. Retracement.
   d. Trading sideways.

23. Which line can be used for short term profit-taking?
   a. 1
   b. 2
   c. 3
   d. 4

24. Which point might represent a weakening trend?
   a. 5
   b. 6
   c. 7
   d. 8

25. If the difference between a channel line and a trendline has been $5 and an upward breakout occurs, prices will likely climb approximately how far above the channel line?
   a. $2.50
   b. $5.00
   c. $10.00
   d. Cannot be estimated.

Refer to the following chart to answer questions 27–30:

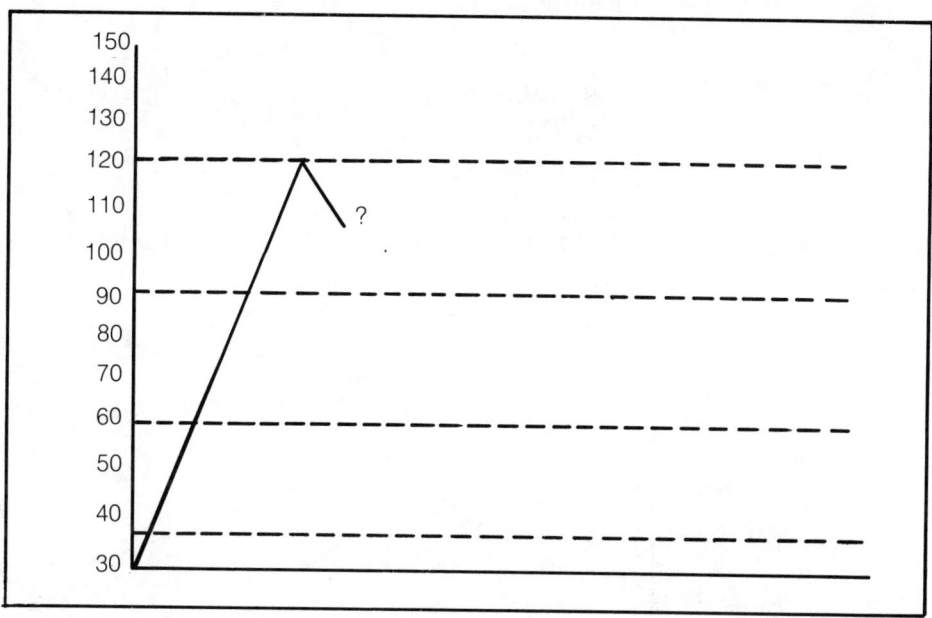

26. The downward-sloping line with the question mark represents a:
   a. Down trendline.
   b. Down tick.
   c. Retracement.
   d. Speedline.

27. If the line went down to the 60 level, the retracement would be:
   a. 33%
   b. 50%
   c. 66%
   d. 60%

28. If the line dropped below the 60 level, you should be thinking in terms of a:
   a. Trend reversal.
   b. Buying area.
   c. Sideways trend.
   d. None of the above.

LESSON THREE

29. If the line does not pass through the 90 level, you should be thinking in terms of a:
- **a.** Trend reversal.
- **(b.)** Buying area.
- **c.** Sideways trend.
- **d.** Short sale.

Refer to the following chart to answer questions 30–31:

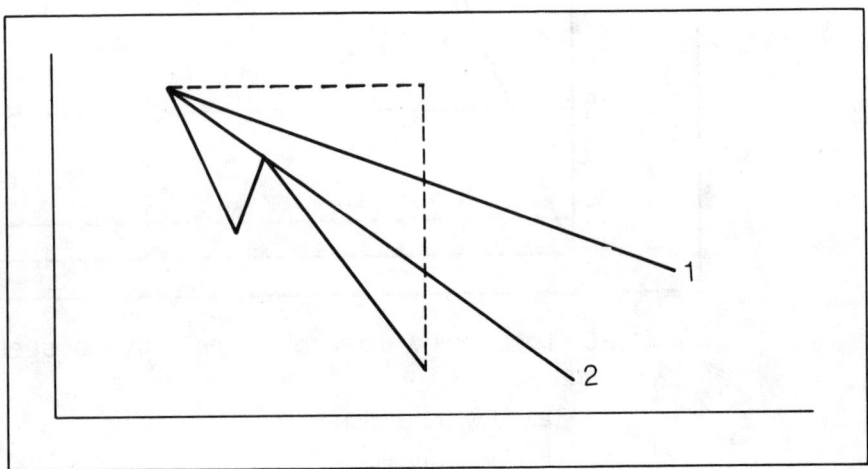

30. Lines 1 and 2 are:
- **a.** Retracement lines.
- **b.** Trendlines.
- **(c.)** Speedlines.
- **d.** Corrections.

31. Which is not true of line 1?

(a.) It represents a retracement of 66%.

b. It is "slower" than line 2.

c. If prices break through line 2, they will probably rally to line 1.

d. It may move through price action when being plotted.

Refer to the following chart to answer questions 32–34:

a.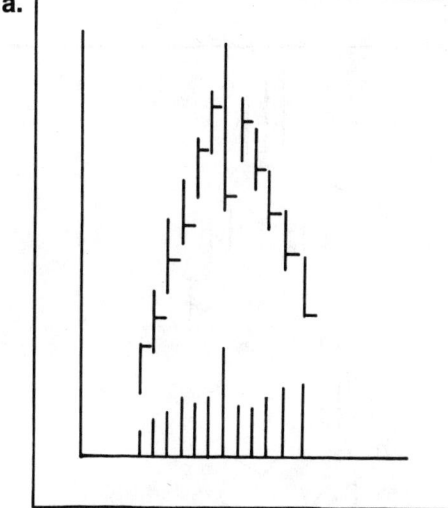

b.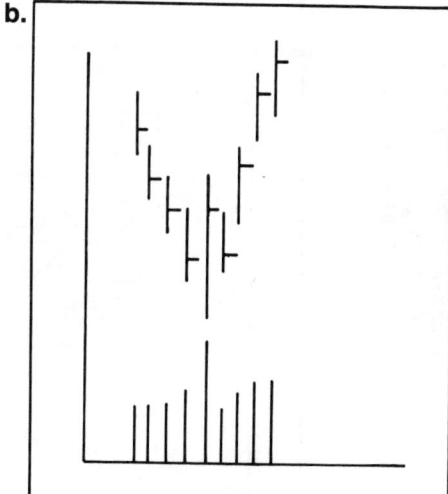

c.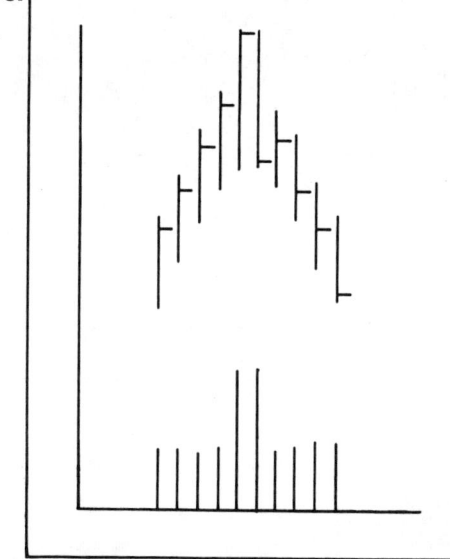

d.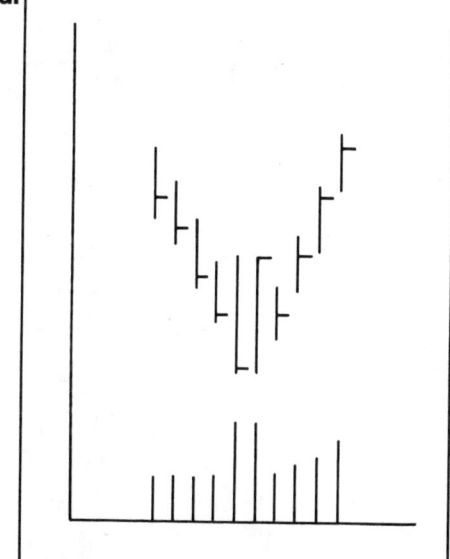

LESSON THREE

<u>a</u> **32.** Which chart shows a top reversal day?
<u>d</u> **33.** Which is an example of a two-day reversal bottom?
<u>b</u> **34.** In all four charts, volume at each reversal point is:
   a. Light.
   b. Heavy.
   c. Moderate.
   d. Cannot be determined.

Refer to the following chart to answer questions 35–38:

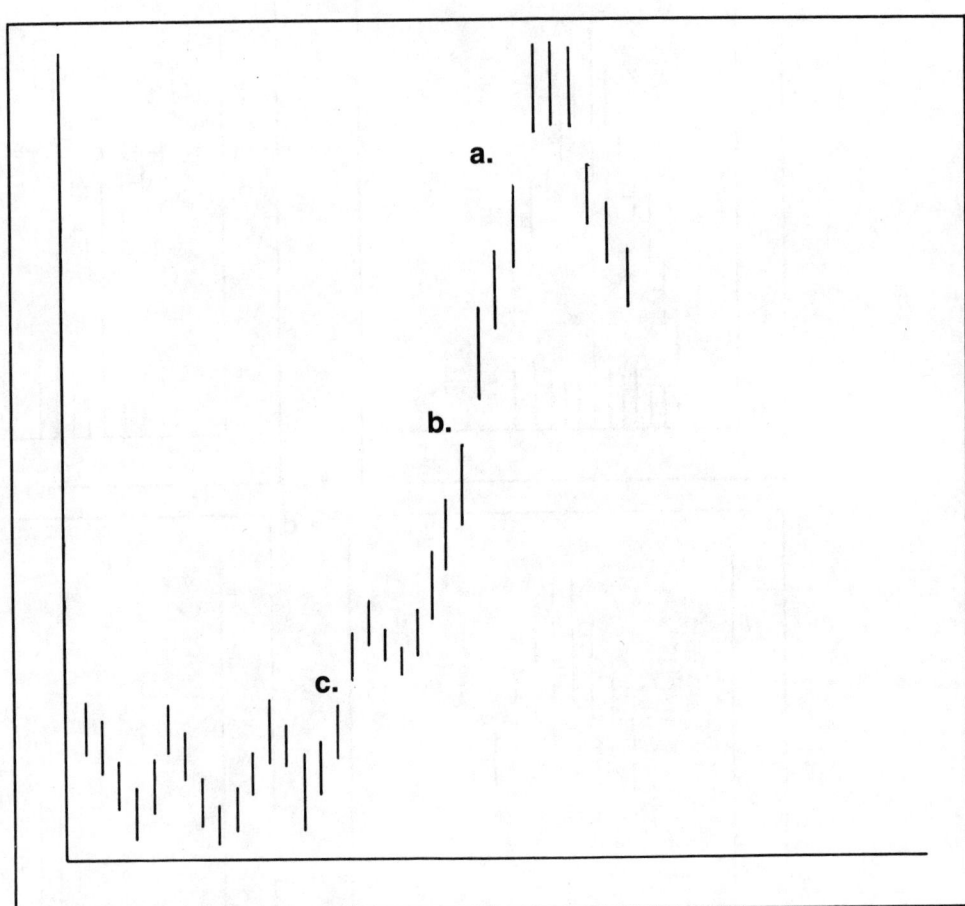

35. Which gap usually occurs on heavy volume and means that a price pattern has been completed? c

36. Which gap usually occurs on moderate volume about halfway through a trend? b

37. The filling of which gap has bearish implications? a

38. The peak of this pattern is called a (an):
- **a.** Correction.
- **b.** Hidden gap.
- **(c.)** Island reversal.
- **d.** Downside breakaway gap.

Answer Sheet

MATCHING QUIZ

21	11	15	7
3	17	6	5
18	4	16	2
6	12	20	2
1	19	2	9
13	14	9	8

MULTIPLE CHOICE

1. c Compare this chart with Figure 4.1 c on page 54.

2. a Compare this chart with Figure 4.1a on page 54.

3. c A market that moves neither up nor down, but rather sideways (or horizontally), is said to be trendless. (See the bottom of p. 55.)

4. c Support is an area below the market, and resistance is a level above the market (see p. 59). Retracement is a countertrend (see pp. 89–91). For an explanation of the correct answer, see page 55.

5. d "intra-day" means "within a day." The time calibration on chart d is in hours; the scales of all the other charts are in units of days, weeks, or months.

6. c This chart shows no trend. Is the market going to break out of the trading range upwards or downwards? It is almost impossible to tell on the basis of the chart above.

7. a Answers b and d are wrong because b describes resistance, which causes prices to turn downward. A support level reflects superior buying pressure, which turns prices upwards (see p. 59). If buying and selling pressures are about equal, the market will move up and down within a narrow trading range, defined by a resistance level at the top and a support level at the bottom. See page 55.

8. a As for answer b, superior buying pressure constitutes support, not resistance (see p. 59). Alternative c is wrong, since both support and resistance can be penetrated (see pp. 64–67). The last statement, d, has to be wrong because the fundamental principle of technical analysis is that the market determines price levels; the chartist merely records them and interprets their movements.

9. b Compare these lines with those in Figure 4.4, page 61.

10. c Once penetrated, support becomes resistance, and resistance becomes support. See pages 64–67. The terms "corrective" and "retracement" both refer to reversals in trend direction; the word "continuous" has to do with a trend's "continuing" in its present direction. None of the latter three terms has anything to do with support or resistance.

11. b First of all, the trend is distinctly upward, not downward. So answers a and d are incorrect. Further, trading ranges are defined between lines a and b and again between lines c and d; so alternative c is incorrect.

12. b Lines e and f clearly penetrate resistance areas indicated by lines a and c. No other lines do that. See pages 64–67.

13. c See page 63. Open interest is an indication of liquidity, not of buying or selling pressure.

14. c A sell stop *is* appropriate in this situation. Should prices dip below $300 and "set off" the sell stop order, you limit your loss. If you place it at or above $300, the order could be executed prematurely. See the bottom of page 67.

15. d The right-hand chart is one of an uptrend. Uptrend lines are always drawn below the price action. Line c is a channel line. See Figure 4.6a on page 68 and Figure 4.17 on page 86.

16. a The left-hand chart shows a downtrend in prices. Down trendlines are always drawn above the price action. Line b is a channel line. See Figure 4.7b on page 71 and Figure 4.17 on page 86.

17. b Once an uptrendline is established (hence points 2 and 4 are not included in the answer), the buying points are whenever prices are near or at the support level (the dashed line). See page 71, particularly Figure 4.7a.

18. c The movement of prices to point 12 represents a significant breaking of the uptrend. No other low does that.

19. d See pages 73–75. Clearly, a brief penetration during the trading day does not constitute a reversal.

20. b Note the angles of the trendlines 1, 2, and 3. Line 1 is pretty close to 45 degrees, a moderate upward rate. Lines 2 and 3 are progressively "flatter," indicating that the uptrend may be weakening. See pages 79–80.

21. c The breaking of the third trendline is a pretty sure indication that prices are headed downward. See pages 77–79.

22. b Compare the diagram with Figure 4.11a on page 77.

23. d The dashed line 4 is a channel line that runs parallel to uptrendline 1. Points 5, 6, and 7 reflect times to sell long positions or to enter short positions. See page 86.

24. d The peak at point 8 failed to test the channel line. See page 86.

25. b Usually the extent of the breakout is roughly the same as the width of the trading ranges before the breakout. See page 87.

26. c The first alternative cannot be right inasmuch as it is not enough of a reversal to establish a downtrend. A "down tick" is just one transaction—at a lower price than that of the previous transaction. A speedline is a line that measures the rate of a trend, not part of the trend (see pp. 91–93). Rather, this line represents a temporary reversal of an uptrend, or a retracement (see pp. 88–91).

27. c The line would "retrace" 66% of the trend (see Figure 4.20a on p. 89). The trend has endured from 30 to 120—90 points. If it drops to 60, that's a 60-point drop, or 66% (60 divided by 90).

LESSON THREE

28. a A retracement of more than 66% generally means the trend has reversed. In this case, buying would not be a profitable tactic, and the trend is certainly not sideways. See page 89.

29. b If prices turn upward again at 90, the retracement is 33%. (That's a 30-point drop divided by a 90-point trend.) The area between 90 (33%) and 75 (50%) is a good buying area (see p. 89).

30. c Compare this chart with Figure 4.21 b on page 92.

31. a Line 1 is "slower" because its angle of descent is less; b is true. So is answer c (see p. 93). Speedlines, unlike trendlines, may be plotted through price action (see p. 91). Alternative a is not true; speedlines do not measure retracement.

32. a See Figure 4.22a, page 94.

33. d See Figure 4.23b, page 96.

34. b Note how volume bars for reversal days are noticeably higher than on the days before and after the reversal. Heavy volume typically accompanies key reversal days. See page 95.

35. c This is a breakaway gap (see p. 98).

36. b This is a runaway, or measuring, gap (see p. 99).

37. a This is an exhaustion gap (see p. 101).

38. c Compare this chart with Figure 4.24a on page 100. See text, pages 101–102.

LESSON FOUR

Major Reversal Patterns and Continuation Patterns

READING ASSIGNMENT

Chapters 5 and 6 of the text.

OBJECTIVES

- Identify the five most commonly used major reversal patterns.
- Distinguish between reversal and continuation patterns.
- Identify continuation patterns such as triangles, flags and pennants, saucers, and wedges.
- Understand the importance of volume pattern and measuring implications.
- Read charts using price information.

READING ORIENTATION

In Chapters 5 and 6 you will study chart patterns. As will become evident, the patterns reviewed build on concepts discussed in the previous chapters. Central to Lesson 4 are the implications that price patterns have in forecasting transition periods. Therefore, price patterns can have predictive value when they appear on the price charts of commodities or stocks.

KEY TERMS

apex, 138
base, 138
bull trap, 125
complex head and shoulders pattern, 116
continuation pattern, 136
double-bottom, 121
flag and pennants, 156
flag pole, 158
head and shoulders top, 109
height, 111
maximum objective, 112
measuring technique, 104
measured move, 167
neckline, 109
price patterns, 104
return move, 110
saucer, 128
spike top, 130
snap back, 133
symmetrical triangle, 139
triangles, 137
volume pattern, 166
wedge, 160
whipsaws, 126

Challenge

MATCHING QUIZ

___10___ apex
_____ base
_____ bull trap
_____ complex head and shoulder pattern
_____ continuation pattern
_____ double-bottom
_____ flags and pennants
_____ flag pole
_____ head and shoulders top
_____ maximum objective
_____ neckline
_____ price patterns
_____ return move
_____ saucer
_____ spike top
_____ snap back
_____ symmetrical triangle
_____ triangles
_____ volume
_____ wedge
_____ whipsaws

1. Often referred to as a "W."
2. The head is higher than either shoulder.
3. A false breakout.
4. Market advances or declines are divided into two equal and parallel moves.
5. A sideways price movement between two parallel horizontal lines.
6. Patterns where two heads or a double left and right shoulder may appear.
7. A nonpattern.
8. A coil.
9. Preceded by a sharp almost straight uptrend.
10. Intersection point at the right where two trendlines meet.
11. Formations or pictures on price charts.
12. An overextended rubber-band effect.
13. The size of the prior market move.
14. A bounce back.
15. In a triangle, the vertical line at the left that measures the pattern height.
16. Data that may help distinguish continuation or reversal patterns.
17. Used in determining minimum price objectives.
18. Where pennants and flags "fly at half-mast."
19. A pattern with a noticeable slant.
20. Generally a line with a slight upward slope at the top.
21. Geometric continuation patterns of which there are three types.
22. Sideways price action that is a pause in prevailing trends.
23. A very slow and gradual trend change.
24. False signals.
25. A method used to arrive at the price objective.

LESSON FOUR

FILL-INS

1. Measuring techniques help to determine the _____ _____ _____.

2. In a head and shoulders top pattern, there are ____ peaks.

3. In a valid head and shoulders top, once the neckline is broken, a subsequent close above the neckline is often called a ____ ____ ____ _____.

4. A symmetrical triangle represents a _____ in the existing trend.

5. In an uptrend resumption, the _____ in volume is essential in all consolidation patterns.

6. In a _____ _____, the two trendlines diverge.

7. The principal of _____ is used to ensure that technical signals and indicators point in the same direction.

8. In a reversal pattern, _____ is more important on the upside price breakout.

9. One of the most reliable and best known reversal patterns is the ____ ____ _____.

10. A failure in confirmation of technical indicators is known as _____.

MULTIPLE CHOICE

1. The following is not common of reversal patterns:
    a. The existence of a prior trend.
    b. The smaller the pattern the greater the subsequent move.
    c. Bottoms usually take longer to build than tops.
    d. All of the above.
2. The maximum objective is a:
    a. 100% retracement.
    b. 76% retracement.
    c. 0% retracement.
    d. 66% retracement.

3. In a "V" or spike reversal which of the following are true statements?
   I. It is a common pattern.
   II. The pattern is easily recognized.
   III. The market "turns on a dime."
   IV. It represents a gradual change.
   a. I only.
   b. II and III.
   c. I and IV.
   d. I and III.

Refer to the following figure to answer questions 4 and 5:

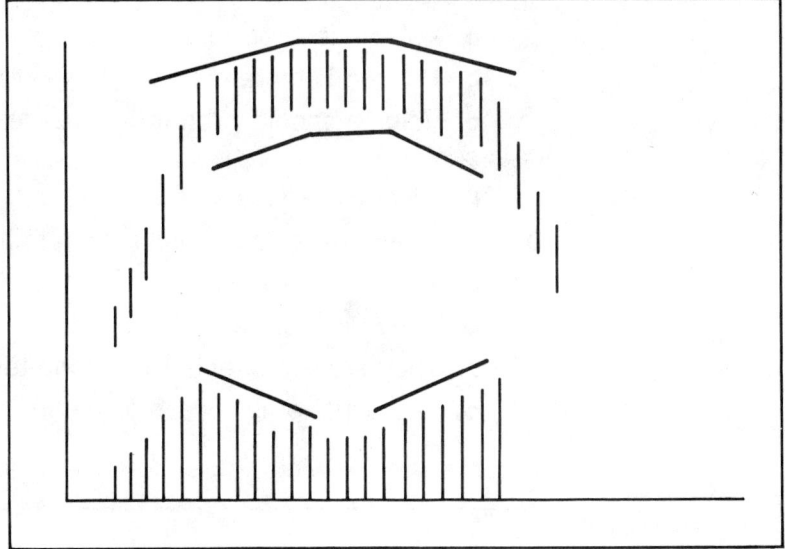

4. This is an example of a:
   a. "V" reversal.
   b. Saucer top.
   c. Nonpattern.
   d. Platter.

5. Which is not a true statement?
   a. This is a common pattern.
   b. It usually occurs at market bottoms.
   c. The trend change is slow and gradual.
   d. Volume diminishes at tops and bottoms.

6. Of the major reversal patterns the most common are:
   a. Head and shoulders, "V," and saucers.
   b. Head and shoulders, double tops and bottoms, and "V."
   c. "V," triple tops and bottoms, and the fan.
   d. Saucers, extended "V," and rectangles.

7. Which is not an example of a continuation pattern?
   a. Triangle.
   b. Rectangle.
   c. Pennant.
   d. Bowl.

8. Which of the following is (are) characteristic of a head and shoulders top?
   a. Volume is important, as it is in all price patterns.
   b. Volume is more critical at market bottoms.
   c. Volume should probably increase for a new downtrend to continue.
   d. All of the above.

9. Which best describes continuation patterns?
   a. There is sideways price action.
   b. They take longer to build.
   c. They are representative of long-term patterns.
   d. These patterns always signal the onset of a new trend.

Refer to the following figures to answer questions 10–13:

Figure I

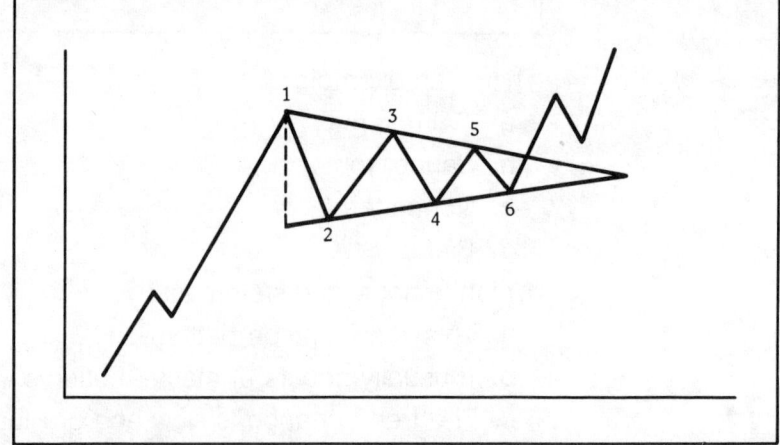

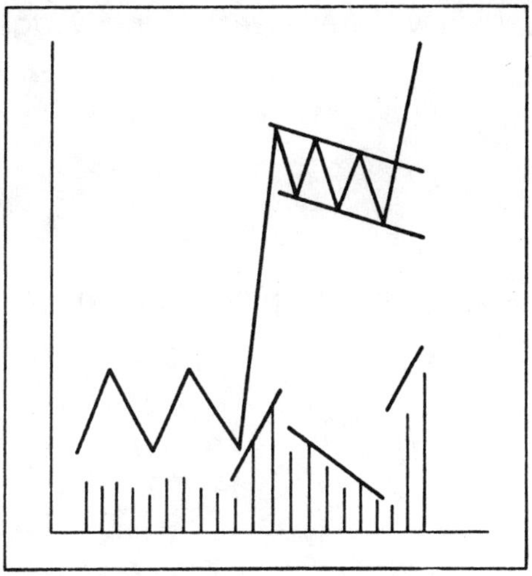

Figure II

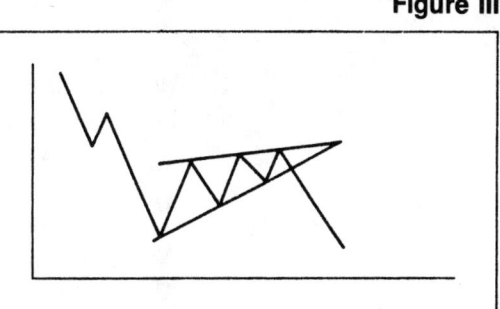

Figure III

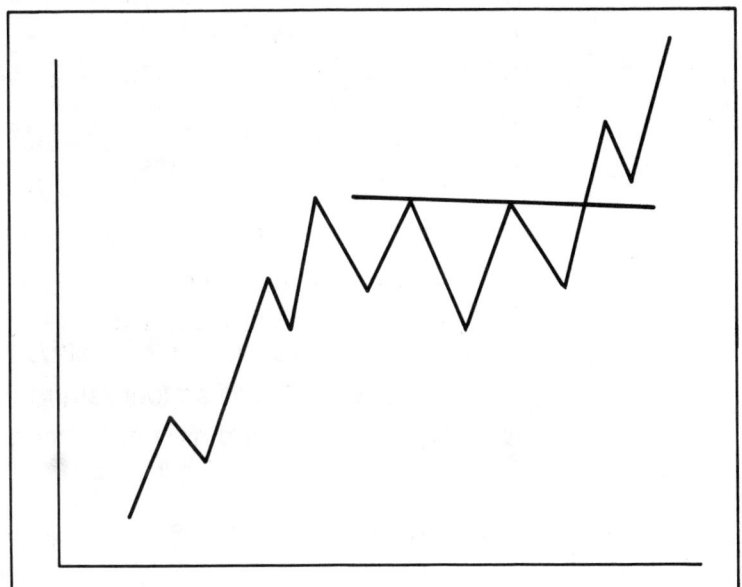

Figure IV

10. For this information pattern to occur a minimum of four reversal points is required.

    a. I
    b. II
    c. III
    d. IV

LESSON FOUR

11. Which pattern is indicative of a bearish rising wedge?
   a. I
   b. II
   c. III
   d. IV

12. Which pattern(s) is (are) an example(s) of a bullish continuation head and shoulders?
   a. I and IV
   b. II
   c. IV
   d. II and III

13. Which pattern is preceded by a sharp line move?
   a. I
   b. II
   c. III
   d. IV

14. Which statement is true? In a valid double top:
   a. There are two distinguishable peaks at very different price levels.
   b. Volume is lighter during the first peak.
   c. Sometimes as many as four return moves occur.
   d. Height is often used as a measuring technique.

Refer to the following figure to answer questions 15 and 16:

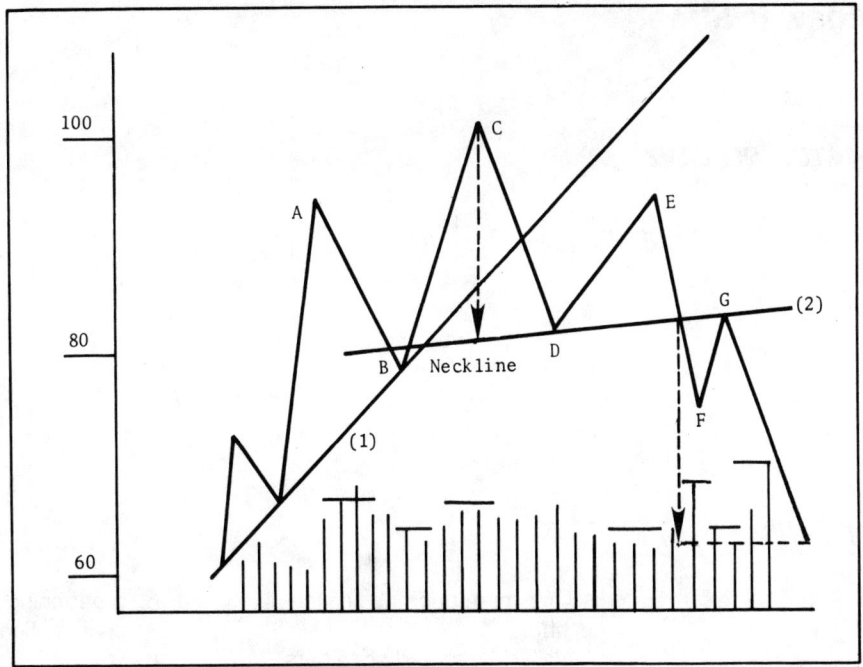

15. In this very common reversal pattern, the return move between F and G will:
   a. Occur on extremely high volume.
   b. Always exceed point E.
   c. Usually not recross the neckline once it's broken.
   d. Always be accompanied by a new trend.

16. This figure is an example of a:
   a. Head and shoulders bottom.
   b. Triple top.
   c. Double top.
   d. Head and shoulders top.

LESSON FOUR

Answer Sheet

MATCHING QUIZ

10	18	7
15	2	12
3	13	8
6	20	21
22	11	16
1	14	19
9	23	24

FILL-INS

1. minimum price objective
2. three
3. failed head and shoulders
4. pause
5. increase
6. broadening formation
7. confirmation
8. volume
9. head and shoulders
10. divergence

MULTIPLE CHOICE

1. b Common to all reversal trends is a need for a prior trend, the breaking of important trendlines, topping and bottom patterns—of which bottoms take longer to build, and the larger the price pattern the greater the subsequent move.

2. a The maximum objective is a 100% retracement of a previous bull market. The 66% retracement may provide significant support under the market.

3. d This pattern is not uncommon. It is often marked by an abrupt reversal trend with little forewarning. It is also one of the most difficult patterns to recognize.

4. b This figure is an example of a saucer top. It represents a slow gradual change in a trend.

5. a This is a fairly infrequent pattern. B, C, and D are common characteristics of saucers.

6. b In choices A and D, saucers are rare and the rectangle is usually a continuation pattern. There is no such thing as a fan in either reversal or continuation patterns.

7. d A bowl is another word used to describe a saucer that is a reversal pattern.

8. d All of the statements are applicable to a head and shoulders top.

9. a Continuation patterns usually are short-term in duration, take shorter periods of time to build, and generally are only a pause in the prevailing trend.

10. a   This is an example of a bullish symmetrical triangle. The minimum requirement for such a formation is four reversal points. However, most have six reversal points as shown in this figure.

11. c   A falling wedge is usually bullish. It is characterized by two converging trendlines with the slope against the prevailing trend.

12. c   This pattern is somewhat similar to a sideways rectangle except that the middle trough in the uptrend is generally lower than the two shoulders.

13. b   This is an example of a bullish flag. It usually occurs after a sharp move and as continuation patterns go, this represents a pause in the trend.

14. d   There are two distinguishable peaks but they usually are at similar price levels. Volume tends to be heavier on the first peak, lighter on the second. Several return moves would not be reflective of a valid top and head pattern.

15. c   If prices do recross the neckline the technician should be alert to the possibility that a failed head and shoulders pattern exists.

16. d   This is an example of the classic head and shoulders top. This is the best known major reversal pattern. Most of the other reversal patterns are just variations of this pattern.

LESSON FIVE

Volume and Open Interest

READING ASSIGNMENT

        Chapter 7 of the text.

OBJECTIVES

- Understand the importance of volume and open interest as secondary indicators.
- Distinguish between OBV and VA lines.
- Read and understand the usefulness of open interest figures in the Commitments of Traders Report.
- Understand how volume and open interest are used to detect trend changes.

READING ORIENTATION

The emphasis of this chapter is directed at helping the reader understand and recognize the importance of volume and open interest as trend indicators. With the conclusion of Chapter 7 the reader will have covered an essential and significant portion of the body of technical analysis.

KEY TERMS

open interest, 179
seasonal tendency, 179
OBV, 185
volume accumulation, 190
blowoffs, 199
large hedgers, 201
"smart money," 201
buyers and sellers, 179
liquidation, 194
selling climaxes, 199
CFTC, 200
small traders, 201

Challenge

MATCHING QUIZ

___6___ open interest

_____ seasonal tendency

_____ OBV

_____ volume accumulation

_____ blowoffs

_____ large hedgers

_____ "smart money"

_____ buyers and sellers

_____ liquidation

_____ selling climaxes

_____ CFTC

_____ smaller traders

1. A three-month perpetual contract.
2. Odd lotters.
3. Voluntary or involuntary close of a position.
4. Large traders are theoretically better informed.
5. A sudden price drop after a long market decline and large decline in open interest.
6. The total number of outstanding longs or shorts.
7. Shows five year open interest average.
8. A sudden price rally and notable decline in open interest.
9. Granville's volume indicator.
10. Commitments of Traders Report.
11. A contract must have both.
12. The most successful group in calling market turns.
13. A neckline slope.
14. A sensitive intra-day percentage volume indicator.

LESSON FIVE

FILL-INS

1. _____ is the most important of the three indicators.
2. In a down trend, declining open interest is _____.
3. The number of contracts traded during a specific time period is called _____.
4. _____ is a simple line indicator used to measure the volume pressure direction.
5. In open interest contracts there are groups of _____ and _____.
6. The total number of outstanding contracts is referred to as _____.
7. For purposes of forecasting, only the _____ volume and open interest are used.
8. The OBV line generally utilizes the number _____ as its starting point.
9. Open interest can be affected in three ways. It can _____, _____, _____ _____ _____.
10. If both parties liquidate old positions, then the open interest should _____.
11. Open interest is accompanied by either a _____ or _____ number.
12. In an uptrend, rising open interest would be considered a _____ sign.
13. Open interest requires _____ adjustments.

MULTIPLE CHOICE

1. In general, if volume and open interest increase then the current trend will:

    a. Usually continue in the same direction.
    b. Reverse.
    c. Signal an end to the current price trend.
    d. None of the above.

Refer to the following figure to answer question 2:

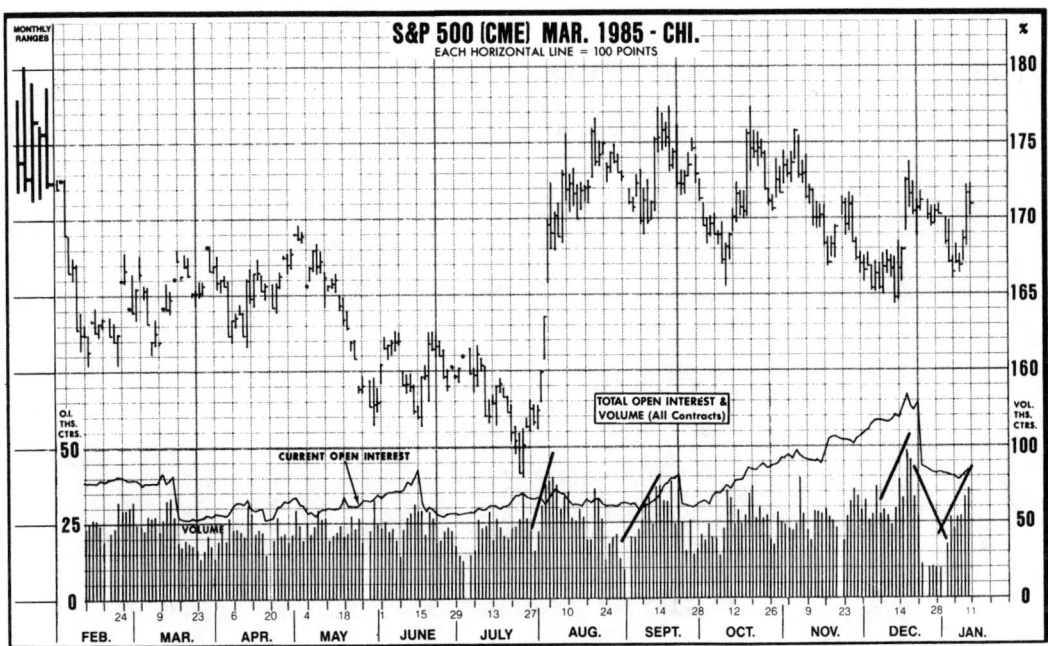

2. Which of the following statement(s) is (are) true?

    I. The period from late July shows a bullish trend.
    II. There is a surge in volume in mid-December.
    III. There is heavy volume during the December correction.
    IV. This figure exemplifies volume following different trends.

    a. I and III.
    b. II, III and IV.
    c. I, II and IV.
    d. I, II and III.

LESSON FIVE

3. The formula $[[(C - L) - (H - C)]/(H - L)] \times V$ is used to construct which line?
  a. On balance volume line.
  b. Inverse trend line.
  c. Compu-Trac line.
  d. Volume accumulation line.

4. Declining open interest in a downward:
  a. Is bearish.
  b. Is bullish.
  c. Reflects a pause in the trend.
  d. Is very rare.

5. Which most accurately describes a danger signal at bull market tops?
  a. An unusually high open interest.
  b. Prices remaining in an uptrend.
  c. All longs have winning positions.
  d. None of the above.

6. Open interest requires:
  a. Three-month adjustments.
  b. No adjustments.
  c. Seasonal adjustments.
  d. Bi-yearly adjustments.

7. What does "volume precedes price" mean?
  a. There is no change in the buying or selling pressure.
  b. Pressure to sell is greater than pressure to buy.
  c. Price is less important than volume.
  d. Changes in the pressure to buy or sell are often detected in the volume before price.

8. What is OBV?
  a. Odd balance volume.
  b. On balance volume.
  c. Off-balance volume.
  d. On balance variation.

9. What does it mean when OBV is used as an indicator?
    a. It is not a lead indicator for a price move.
    b. It never reflects divergence.
    c. It may be a confirming indicator.
    d. None of the above.

Refer to the following figure to answer question 10:

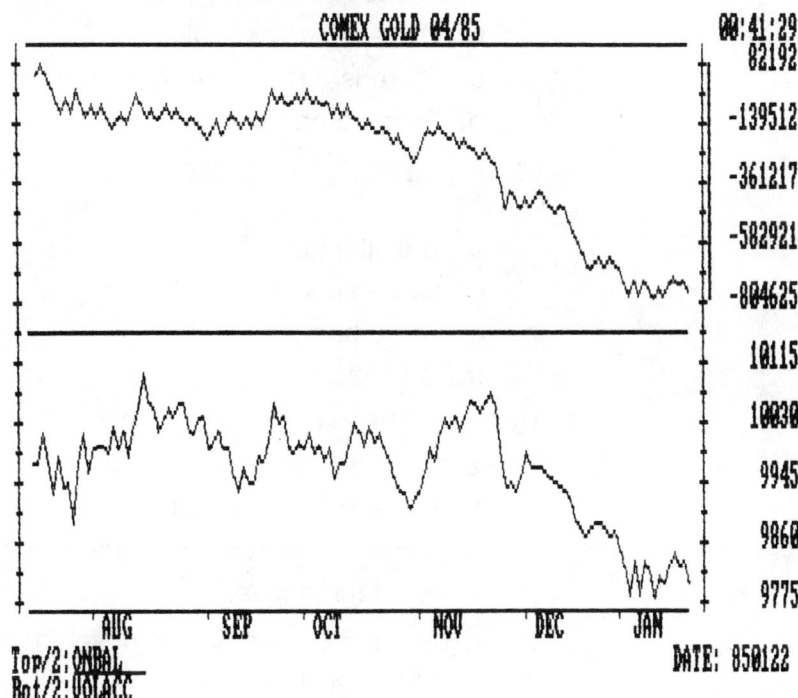

10. This figure shows the:
    a. VA line represented at the bottom.
    b. OBV line represented at the top.
    c. VA line seemingly more sensitive than the OBV line.
    d. All of the above.
11. The Commitments of Traders Report:
    a. Shows the open interest statistics of the previous month.
    b. Is released by the Commodity Futures Traders Committee.
    c. Is a new forecasting tool.
    d. Provides daily statistics.

12. Blowoffs are most prevalent:
    a. At major market tops.
    b. In sideways consolidation patterns.
    c. At major market bottoms.
    d. During slow trading.

13. Which is not true of a selling climax?
    a. Prices rise sharply first.
    b. There is heavy trading.
    c. There is a large decline in the open interest.
    d. Prices drop sharply.

14. In general, which group is most successful in calling market turns?
    a. The little guy.
    b. Large speculators.
    c. Large hedgers.
    d. Odd lotters.

15. The OBV line:
    a. Uses a plus or minus value.
    b. Is a volume indicator.
    c. Generally follows the direction of the price trend.
    d. All of the above.

16. Which of these individuals developed OBV?
    a. Marc Chaikin.
    b. James Sibbet.
    c. Joseph Granville.
    d. Charles H. Dow.

Please refer to the following figure to answer question 17:

17. In the figure the OBV line:
    a. Confirms the lower price trend.
    b. Signals a strong bearish trend.
    c. Is moving sideways.
    d. Is not reflective of a trend.

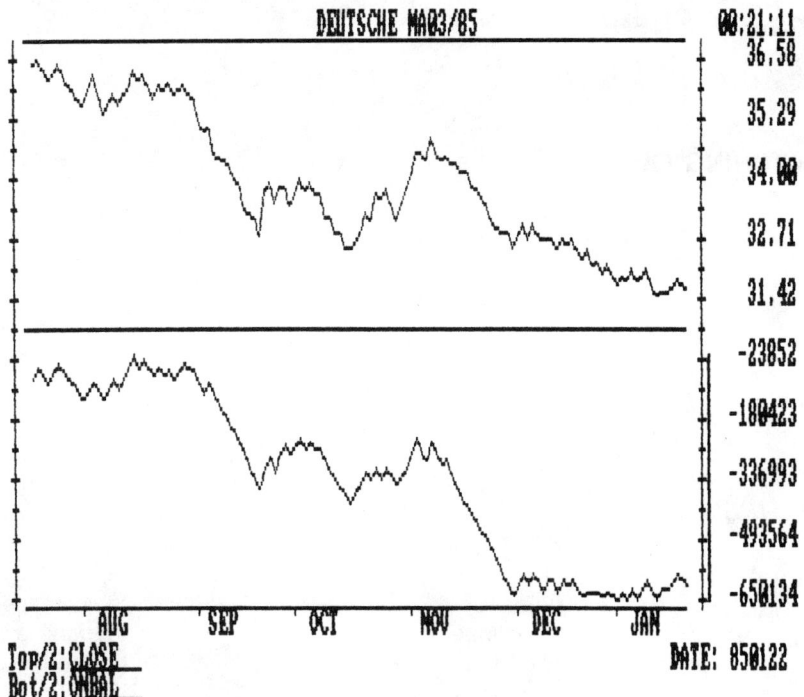

18. Open interest most accurately represents the:
    a. Percentage of shorts and longs divided by two.
    b. Total number of outstanding longs or shorts.
    c. Difference between volume and seasonal tendencies.
    d. One third of the preceding market move.

19. OBV lines attempt to determine whether heavier volume takes place on:
    a. Upside trends.
    b. Downside trends.
    c. Horizontal trends.
    d. A and B only.

20. Rising open interest in a downtrend is:
    a. Bearish.
    b. A poor indicator of market trends.
    c. Bullish.
    d. Reflective of sluggish new short selling.

LESSON FIVE

Answer Sheet

MATCHING QUIZ

6	4
7	11
9	3
14	5
8	10
12	2

FILL-INS

1. Price
2. bullish
3. volume
4. OBV
5. buyers . . . sellers
6. open interest
7. total
8. 10,000
9. increase, decrease, not change
10. decline
11. positive . . . negative
12. bullish
13. seasonal

MULTIPLE CHOICE

1. a Declining volume and open-interest suggest that the present price trend may be ending.

2. c Close inspection of this figure clearly shows light volume after the mid-December surge.

3. d This formula is used to construct the volume accumulation line, where H=High, C=Close, L=Low, and V=Volume.

4. b Declining open interest in an uptrend is bearish, as is declining open interest in a downtrend. It does not reflect a pause in the trend nor is it a very rare occurrence.

5. a A high open interest figure at market tops may even be a bearish signal especially if the price drop is sudden.

6. c Open interest is seasonally adjusted since it has very definite seasonal tendencies that must be taken into consideration.

7. d Price is much more important than volume. There are definite pressures to buy or sell depending on the direction of the prevailing trend.

8. b On balance volume (OBV) is the only correct answer.

9. c When it is used as a co-indicator, it can be a confirming or lead indicator of a price move.

10. d In this split figure the OBV line is at the top, the VA line at the bottom. As it appears, the VA line seems more sensitive in representation.

11. a It is not a new forecasting tool. It is a monthly, not a daily report. The CFTC is the Commodity Futures Trading Commission.

12. a Blowoffs occur at major market tops. Prices generally rise sharply after long advances. There is a concurrent jump in trading activity and a notable decline in open interest.

13. a Prices rise only after a sharp drop first. Selling climaxes occur at market bottoms. Selections B, C, and D are also true statements.

14. c Large hedgers theoretically are the most successful group in calling market turns. Large speculators are second, and the little guy or odd lotter is the least successful.

15. d All of the statements apply to OBV lines.

16. c Marc Chaikin developed the volume accumulation line. This is a sensitive intra-day measure. Sibbet developed the Demand Index, which uses complicated formulas that incorporate volume with price action. Dow first published stock market averages; he is given credit for what is commonly known as the Dow Theory. His theory is the foundation of technical analysis.

17. c This figure represents a sideways moving OBV line. It is not confirming a lower price trend. It may also warn the analyst not to be bearish in forecasting a new trend.

18. b Of the choices available, the most accurate statement is that open interest is the total number of outstanding shorts or longs.

19. d The primary function of the OBV line is to determine whether volume is taking place on the upside or downside.

20. a Rising open interest in an uptrend is a bullish sign. Rising open interest in a downtrend is also reflective of aggressive new short selling.

LESSON SIX

Long-Term Charts and Commodity Indices

READING ASSIGNMENT

Chapter 8 of the text.

OBJECTIVES

- Understand the usefulness of long-term charting.
- Review long-term charts and realize the importance of the historical data they contain.
- Understand the importance of following general commodity indices.

READING ORIENTATION

Chapter 8 discusses the importance of long-term charts for analysis and forecasting purposes. Examples of weekly and monthly charts are plentiful. These charts also provide the reader with a review of concepts and price patterns covered in the previous chapters.

MIDTERM REVIEW

At the end of Lesson 6, you will have an opportunity to collectively assess your knowledge of the various topics and concepts introduced thus far.

KEY TERMS

apex, 138
bar chart, 41
broadening formation, 150
Charles Dow, 24
commodity future, 14
confirmation, 174
continuation patterns, 136
descriptive statistics, 20
divergence, 175
flags and pennants, 156
flow of funds analysis, 16
fundamentalist, 5
head and shoulders, 104
key reversal day, 96
large hedgers, 201
lines, 32
long-term charts, 218
measured move, 167
measuring technique, 104
M.T.A., 24
neckline, 105
OBV, 185
open interest, 44
perpetual contract, 210
price filter, 74
price gaps, 97
price pattern, 104
Random Walk Theory, 20
resistance, 59
relative strength, 216
saucer, 128
seasonal tendency, 179
selling climax, 95
snap back, 133

speedlines, 91
spike, 130
stand aside, 56
support, 59
technician, 5
trend, 53
triangle, 139
volume, 43
whipsaws, 74

When you have completed the reading assignment for Lesson Six, proceed to the Midterm Examination, which includes questions covering Lesson Six material.

Midterm Examination

MATCHING QUIZ

_____ speedlines
_____ support
_____ open interest
_____ bar chart
_____ M.T.A.
_____ price gaps
_____ key reversal day
_____ selling climax
_____ price filter
_____ long-term charts
_____ continuation patterns
_____ flags and pennants
_____ fundamentalists
_____ commodity futures
_____ flow of funds analysis
_____ creation of first Dow Average
_____ lines
_____ volume
_____ technicians
_____ measuring techniques
_____ head and shoulders
_____ spike
_____ descriptive statistics
_____ trend
_____ stand aside

1. Cash position of different groups.
2. A key turning point identified after the fact.
3. Study causes of market movement.
4. Direction of market movement.
5. Reaction lows or troughs.
6. Horizontal trading bands.
7. Part of a head & shoulders pattern.
8. July 3, 1884.
9. Market Technicians Association.
10. Measure trends in terms of rates of ascent or descent.
11. Requiring a trendline be broken by a predetermined price increment.
12. Both a price and time chart.
13. A sudden trend reversal with little forewarning.
14. A sudden turnaround on heavy volume at the bottom of a bear market.
15. Total number of outstanding contracts.
16. Seen in five-year average of open interest.
17. Sudden price rally with a notable decline in open interest.
18. Diverging trendlines that look like an expanding triangle.
19. An open space on a bar chart where no trading has taken place.
20. Over-extended "rubber band" effect.
21. To do nothing.
22. Total amount of trading for a particular market day.
23. General agreement of indicators.
24. Data presented in a graph format.
25. An intersection point at the right where two trendlines meet.
26. Selling pressure is stronger than buying pressure.
27. Help determine long-term major trend and price objectives.
28. Price movement is random and unpredictable.
29. Market advances or declines are divided into two equal and parallel moves.

LESSON SIX

_____ triangle
_____ neckline
_____ confirmation
_____ broadening formation
_____ Random Walk Theory
_____ saucer
_____ whipsaws
_____ resistance
_____ perpetual contract^{tm}
_____ large hedgers
_____ OBV
_____ divergence
_____ measured move
_____ snap back
_____ apex
_____ seasonal tendency
_____ price pattern

30. Usually reflects sideways price action.
31. A line or curving volume indicator.
32. Preceded by a sharp, almost straight line move.
33. A slow gradual change in a trend.
34. A major and common reversal pattern.
35. All are traded on margin.
36. Indicators fail to confirm one another.
37. Study effects of market movement.
38. Bad signals.
39. Aid in determining minimum price objectives.
40. A continuous futures price history.
41. Most successful group in calling market turns.
42. Formation on a price chart.
43. Requires a minimum of four reversal points.

LESSON SIX

FILL-INS

1. A reversal pattern that is characterized by a slow and gradual trend change is called a _____.

2. All futures are traded on _____, usually less than 10%.

3. Technical analysts believe that market action _____ everything.

4. The simplest and best known volume line indicator is _____.

5. _____ and _____ are preceded by almost a straight line move.

6. An abrupt trend reversal with little or no warning, followed by a quick move in the opposite direction is called a _____ pattern.

7. _____ charts are not meant for trading purposes.

8. Market action includes the following principal data sources: _____, _____, _____.

9. The vertical axis on a bar chart represents the _____ of the contract.

10. When interpreting open interest, rising open interest in an uptrend is considered _____.

11. _____ _____ are parallel trendlines drawn over or under the price action.

12. _____ and _____ _____ are reported a day late.

13. The direction of peaks and troughs constitute a _____ _____.

14. "Whipsaws" are _____ _____.

15. Reaction lows are called _____ _____.

16. A _____ _____ or coil is usually a _____ pattern.

17. Only the total _____ and _____ _____ numbers are used for forecasting purposes.

18. An _____ triangle is bullish and _____ triangle is bearish.

19. A long-term _____ chart is linked together by a number of contracts.

20. The _____ _____ provides years of price history on a continuum, as an alternative to using nearby months.

21. The proper order in long-term chart analysis is to begin with the ___ _____ and work toward the ___ ___.

MULTIPLE CHOICE

Please refer to the following figure to answer question 1:

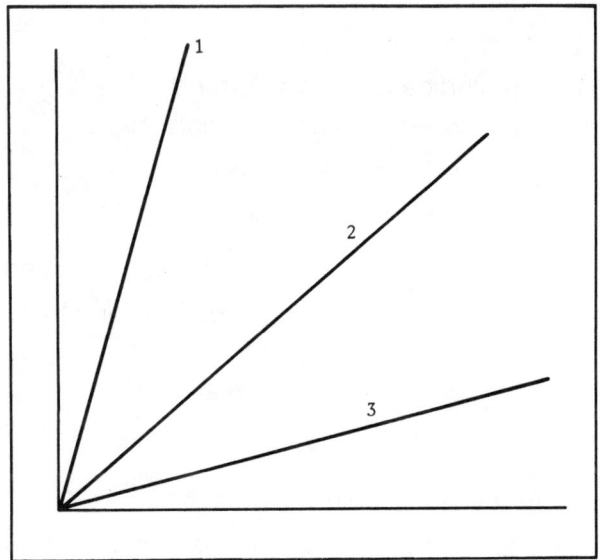

1. The most valid trendline is:
   a. line 1.
   b. line 2.
   c. lines 1 and 3.
   d. None of the above.

Please refer to the following figure to answer question 2:

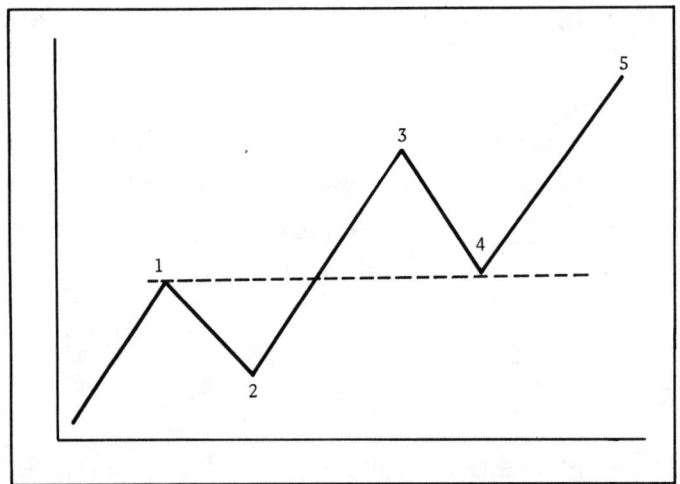

2. Points 1 and 4 are:
    a. Indicative of an uptrend.
    b. Resistance and support levels.
    c. Resistance levels only.
    d. A sideways pattern.

3. The technical analysis approach is based on:
    a. Market action discounting everything.
    b. Prices moving in trends.
    c. History repeating itself.
    d. All of the above.

4. In a valid double top:
    a. There are two distinguishable peaks at very different price levels.
    b. Volume is lighter on the first peak.
    c. Sometimes several bounces occur.
    d. Height is often used as a measuring technique.

Please refer to the following figure to answer question 5:

5. This is an example of a:
   a. Monthly continuation chart.
   b. Weekly continuation chart.
   c. Point and figure chart.
   d. A daily bar chart.

LESSON SIX

Please refer to the following figure to answer question 6:

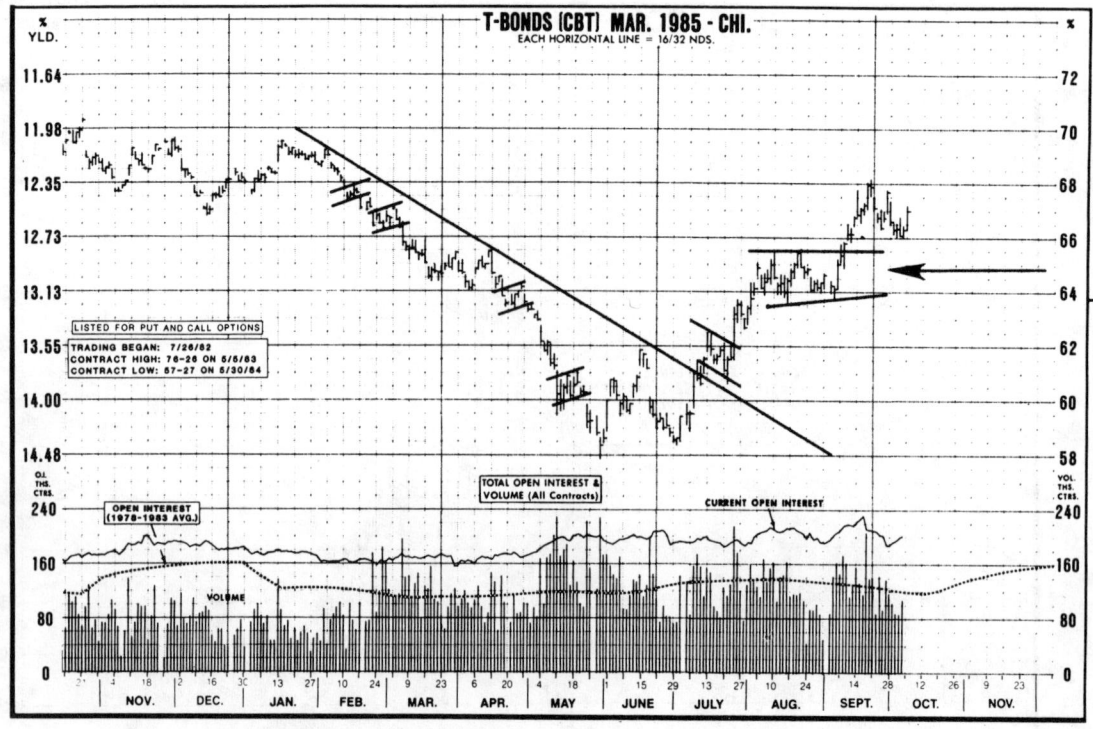

6. During the February to May period, the sloping parallel lines are:
    a. Descending triangles.
    b. Declining pennants.
    c. Rising flags.
    d. Wedges.

Please refer to the following figure to answer question 7:

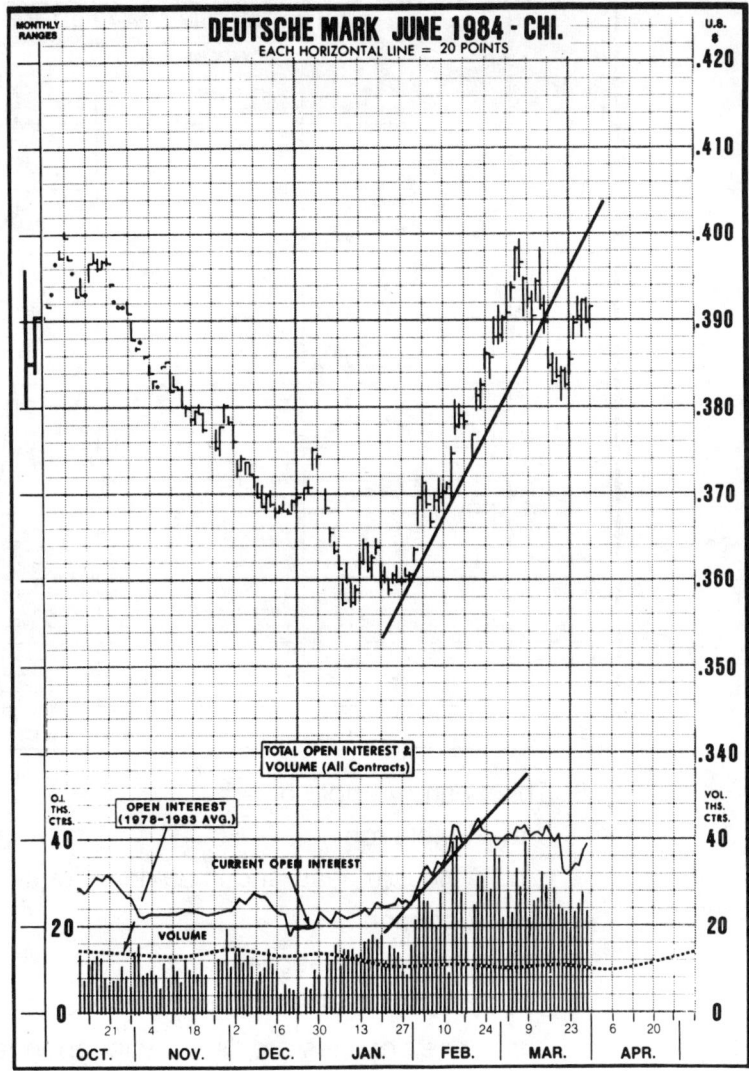

7. In this depiction:
   a. Open interest is giving off false signals.
   b. Declining open interest is bullish.
   c. Rising open interest during February confirmed the rally.
   d. Volume was light on the February upswing.

LESSON SIX

Please refer to the following figure to answer question 8:

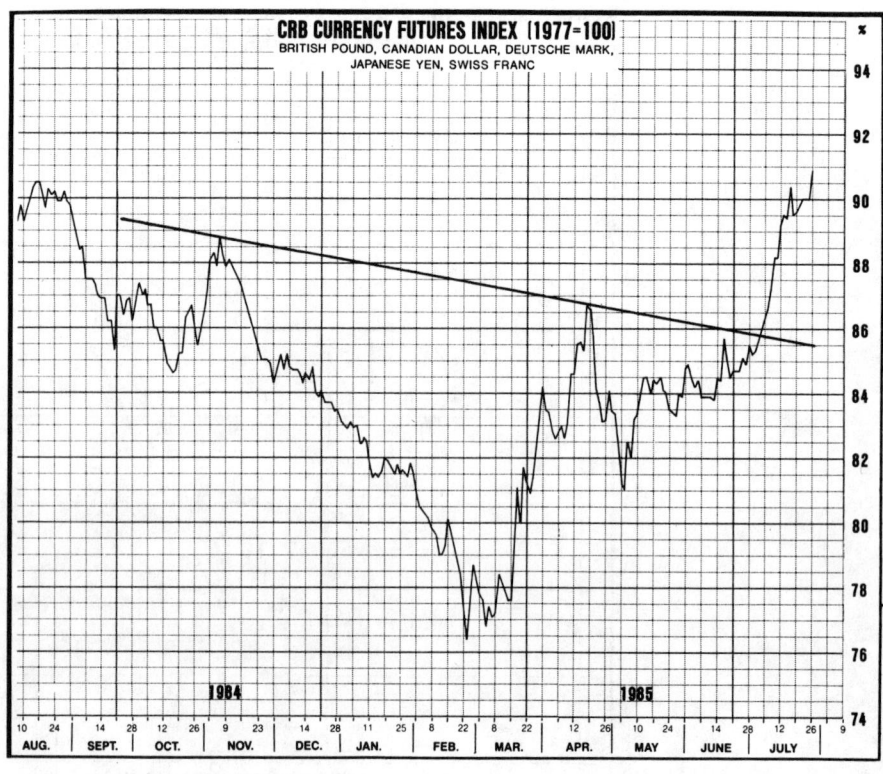

8. This is an example of:
   a. A triple top.
   b. A double head and shoulders bottom.
   c. A diamond.
   d. None of the above.

9. The Random Walk Theorists claim that:
   a. Price changes are "serially independent."
   b. Price changes are predictable.
   c. Buy and hold strategies are useless.
   d. None of the above.

10. According to Dow, market trends have:
    a. Six categories.
    b. Five categories.
    c. Two categories.
    d. Three categories.

11. Which most accurately describes a danger signal in a bull market at market tops.

  a. An unusually high open interest.
  b. Rising open interest in an uptrend.
  c. Prices remaining in an uptrend.
  d. All longs having winning positions.

Please refer to the following figure to answer question 12:

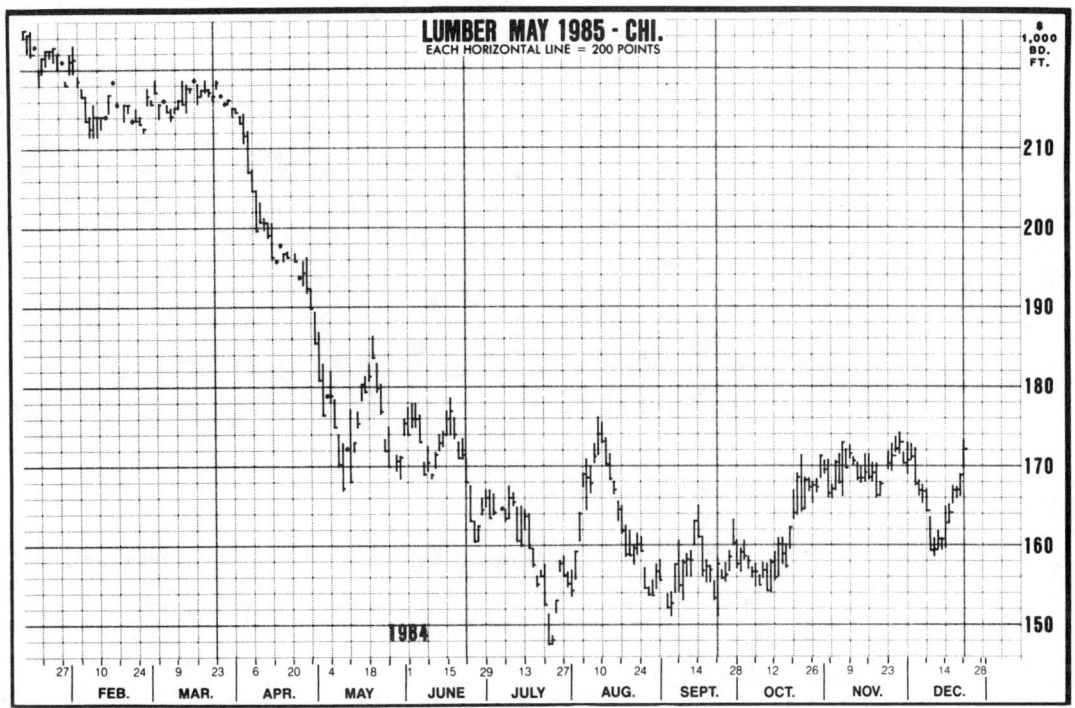

12. This figure represents:

  a. Rising open interest.
  b. A saucer.
  c. A down and sideways trend.
  d. A nonpattern.

13. In order to confirm a trend, volume should:

  a. Reflect an island reversal pattern.
  b. Expand in the direction of the major trend.
  c. Reverse in the direction of the major trend.
  d. Move horizontally in the direction of the major trend.

Please refer to the following figure to answer question 14:

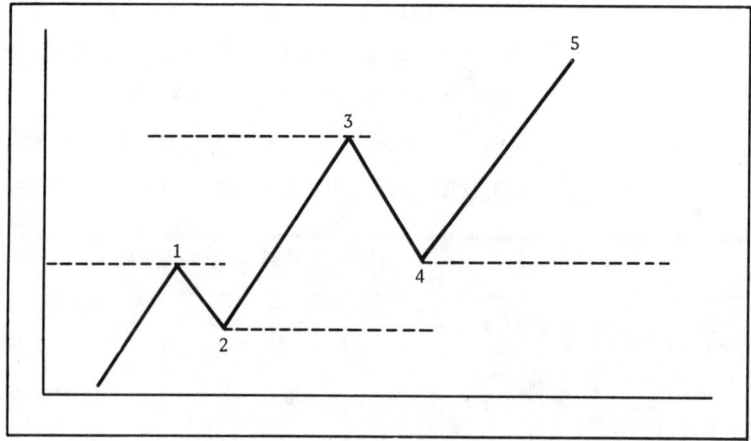

14. Points 1 and 3 are:
   a. Troughs.
   b. Support levels.
   c. Reaction lows.
   d. Resistance levels.

Please refer to the following figure to answer question 15:

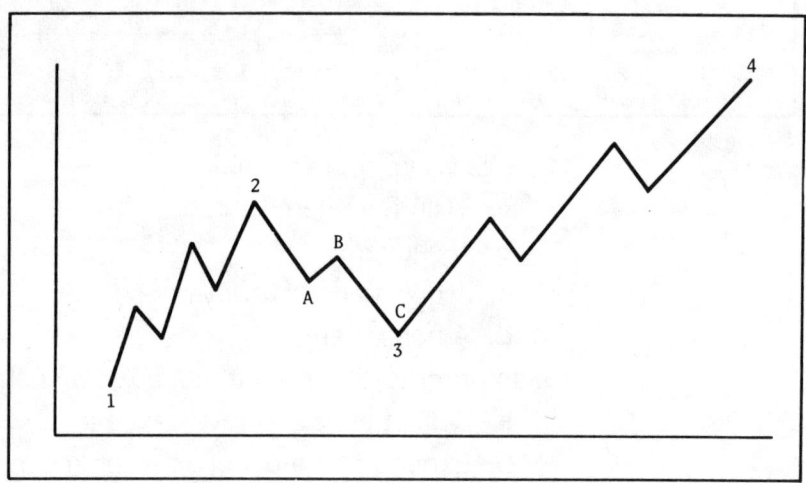

15. Points 1, 2, 3, and 4 show the:
    a. Secondary downtrend.
    b. Major uptrend.
    c. Minor uptrend.
    d. Secondary uptrend.
16. Which is not an example of a continuation pattern?
    a. Triangle.
    b. Rectangle.
    c. Pennant.
    d. Right angle.
17. Which is not true during a selling climax?
    a. Prices rise sharply first.
    b. There is heavy trading.
    c. There is a large decline in open interest.
    d. Prices drop sharply first.

Please refer to the following figure to answer question 18:

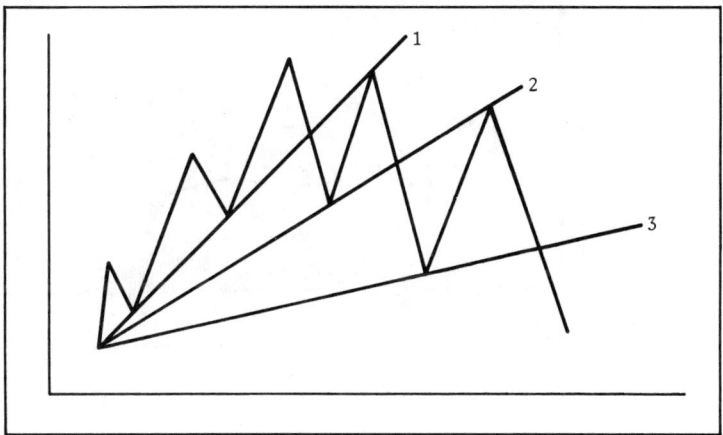

18. This figure depicts the:
    a. Fan principle.
    b. Signal of a trend reversal at point 3.
    c. Trendlines at 1 and 2 becoming resistance lines.
    d. All of the above.

Please refer to the following figure to answer question 19:

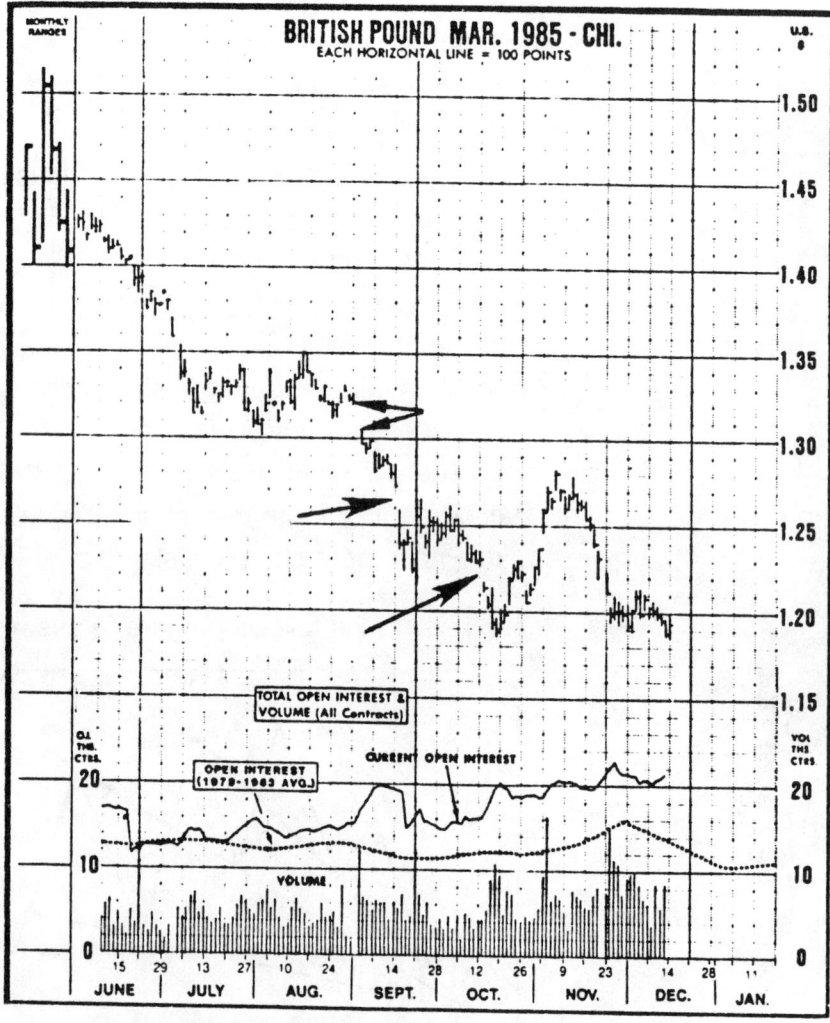

19. The double-headed arrow is the:
   a. Exhaustion gap.
   b. Measuring gap.
   c. Retracement gap.
   d. Breakaway gap.

Please refer to the following figure to answer question 20:

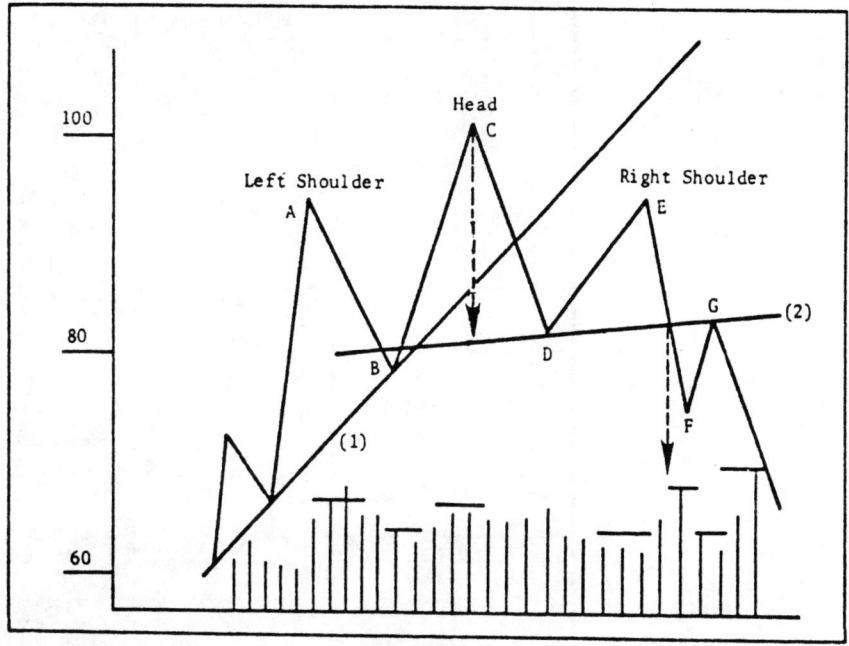

20. The line that forms along B, D, or G is the:
   a. Hairline.
   b. Neckline.
   c. Defensive posture line.
   d. Downward trendline.

LESSON SIX

Please refer to the following figure to answer question 21:

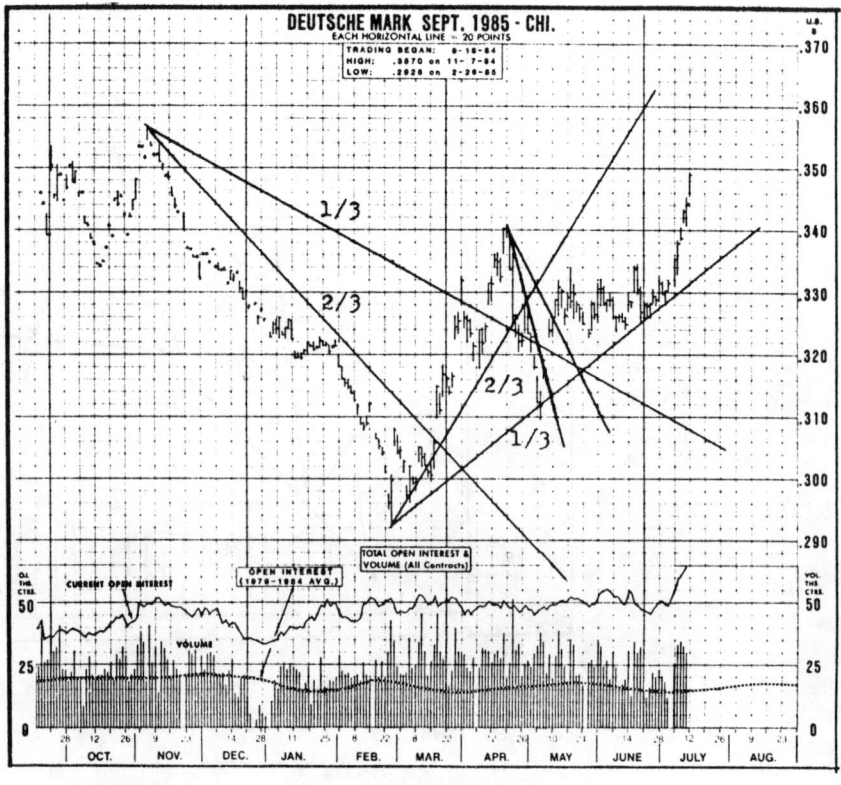

21. In this figure the 1/3 and 2/3 notations are:
    a. Speedlines.
    b. Ratio retracement patterns.
    c. OBV lines.
    d. Height measurements.
22. The following is not common to all reversal patterns:
    a. The existence of a prior trend.
    b. The smaller the pattern, the greater the subsequent move.
    c. Bottoms usually take longer to build.
    d. All of the above.

Please refer to the following figure to answer question 23:

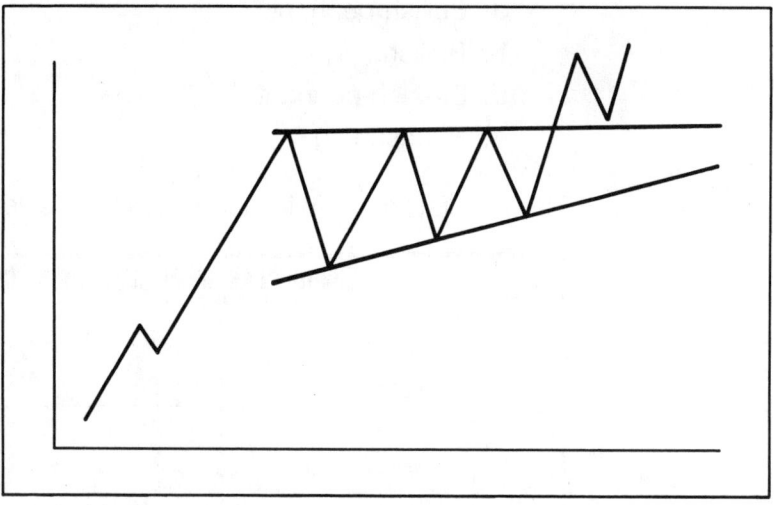

23. This figure represents a:
    a. Bullish descending triangle.
    b. Bearish descending triangle.
    c. Bullish ascending triangle.
    d. Bearish ascending triangle.

Please refer to the following figure to answer question 24:

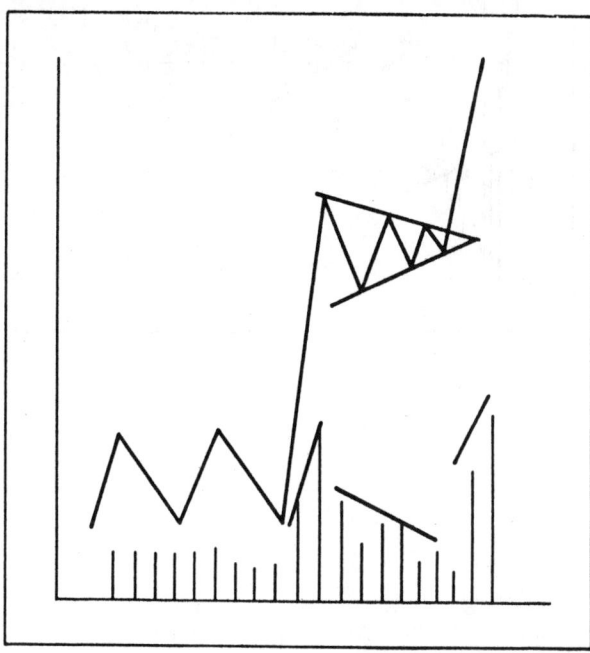

24. This is an example of a:
   a. Bullish pennant.
   b. Bullish flag.
   c. Bearish pennant.
   d. Bearish flag.

Please refer to the following figure to answer question 25:

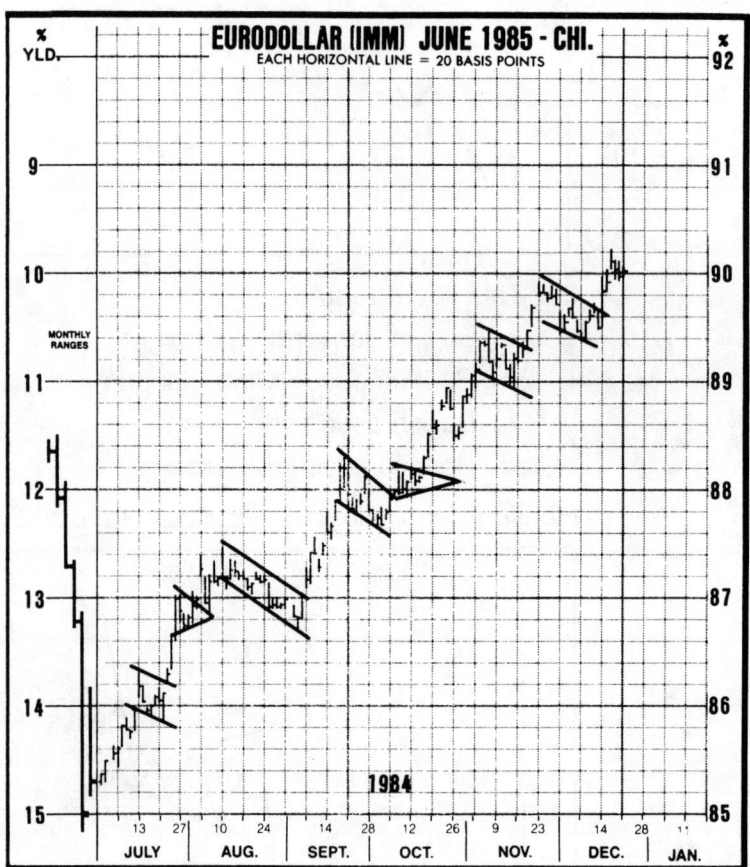

25. In this figure:
- **a.** Flags and pennants are shown.
- **b.** Brief pauses in the trend are shown.
- **c.** Dynamic market moves are reflected.
- **d.** All of the above.

Midterm Answer Sheet

MATCHING QUIZ

10	32	24	26
5	3	4	40
15	35	21	41
12	1	43	31
9	8	7	36
19	6	23	29
2	22	18	20
14	37	28	25
11	39	33	16
27	34	38	42
30	13		

FILL-INS

1. saucer
2. margin
3. discounts
4. OBV
5. Flags . . . pennants
6. V- or spike
7. Long-term
8. price, volume, open interest
9. price
10. bullish
11. Price channels
12. Volume . . . open interest
13. market trend
14. bad signals
15. support levels
16. symmetrical triangle . . . continuation
17. volume . . . open interest
18. ascending . . . descending
19. continuation
20. Perpetual Contract™
21. long range . . . near term

MULTIPLE CHOICE

1. b This is Figure 4.12 (on page 80 in the text). Line 2, which closely approximates a 45-degree angle, is the most valid trendline.

2. b See Figure 4.5a on page 65.

3. d All correctly state the basic premises of the technical approach.

4. d There are two distinguishable peaks but they usually have similar price patterns. Volume tends to be heavy on the first peak, lighter on the second. Several return moves would not be reflective of a valid double top.

5. a This is Figure 3.13, page 50. In this example of a long-term continuation pattern, each bar presents one month.

6. c See Figure 6.3b, page 145. A close inspection of this figure reveals four rising flags. There are no wedges or pennants.

7. c In this figure (p. 195, Figure 7.11a), open interest clearly confirmed the market rally. The upswing was on heavy volume.

8. d This figure represents a head and shoulders bottom. Notice the slope of the neckline. There are no diamond patterns in this figure (p. 115).

9. a Random Walk Theory states that prices are unpredictable, and the simplest strategy to follow is to buy and hold.

10. d Dow identified three categories—the primary, secondary, and minor. Bear in mind that the number three shows up quite frequently in the technical analysis approach. For example, three sources of information—price, volume, and open interest.

11. a A high open interest figure at market tops may even be a bearish signal, especially if the price drop is sudden.

12. c This is Figure 4-1d on page 55. Open interest is not plotted on this figure. Nor is this figure reflective of a saucer or nonpattern.

13. b Most horizontal trends reflect a pause in the market prior to the next upward or downward move. An island reversal pattern in isolation should not be used to predict a major trend move.

14. d See page 59, Figure 4.3a. Points 1 and 3 are resistance levels. Points 2 and 4 are support levels.

15. b These points reflect a major uptrend. A, B, and C are minor waves between points 2 and 3 which in and of itself represents a secondary correction within the uptrend (Figure 4.2a, p. 57).

16. d There is no such thing as a right angle continuation pattern.

17. a Prices drop sharply first. During "blowoffs," prices rise sharply first. B and C are also statements that apply to "selling climaxes."

18. d This is an example (page 77) of the fan principle. Note that trendlines 1 and 2 have become resistance lines, and point 3 signals the trend reversal.

19. d The arrow in the middle of the figure is the measuring gap. The bottom arrow is the exhaustion gap (Figure 4.24b, p. 100).

20. b This is an example of a head and shoulders top. A and E are the shoulders, C is the head, and lines B, D, and G form the neckline.

21. a The 1/3 and 2/3 lines are speedlines. Developed by Edson Gould, speedlines divide the trend into thirds. They measure the rate of ascent or descent of a trend.

22. b Common to all reversal trends is a need for a prior tend, breaking of trendlines, top and bottom patterns—of which bottoms take longer to build; and the larger the price pattern the greater the subsequent move.

23. c This is an example of a continuation pattern that is bullish. Note the rising lower line (p. 138, Figure 6.1b). A bearish pattern would be reflective of a descending triangle.

24. a The bullish pennant resembles a small symmetrical triangle. Pennants and flags represent a brief pause in an otherwise dynamic market (p. 157).

25. d This is a clear example of a dynamic market move with pennants and flags represented. Remember, both patterns are but a brief pause in the trend (p. 158).

LESSON SEVEN

Moving Averages

READING ASSIGNMENT

Chapter 9 of the text.

OBJECTIVES

- Realize the importance of this technical indicator.
- Identify the three different types of moving averages.
- Understand how moving averages are used.
- Understand the concept of the weekly rule technique.

READING ORIENTATION

As the reader explores this chapter, it will become evident that moving averages are widely used and quite informative as a trend-following system. As an indicator they are precise and computer-programmable. A well-rounded background in this area will prove beneficial to the exacting technician.

KEY TERMS

arithmetic mean, 237
center, 257
double crossover method, 247
four week rule, 272
harmonics, 270
high-low band, 244
lead time, 257
linear weighted moving average, 238
moving average, 234
percentage envelopes, 243
settlement price, 237
time filter, 243,
13, 21, 34, 55
5, 10, 20, 40

Challenge

MATCHING QUIZ

__4__ moving average
____ settlement price
____ arithmetic mean
____ percentage envelopes
____ double crossover system
____ triple crossover method
____ center
____ 13, 21, 34, 55
____ 5, 10, 20, 40
____ harmonics
____ lead time
____ high-low band
____ time filter
____ linear weighted moving average

1. 4-19-18 day moving average combination.
2. The moving average applied to high and low prices.
3. A simple breakout system based on the monthly major cycle.
4. Average of a body of data.
5. A statistically correct way to plot a moving average.
6. Total divided by the sum of the multipliers.
7. Simple moving average.
8. A 1- to 3-day delay tactic before taking action.
9. Days often used for moving averages.
10. Price most often used for moving average analysis.
11. Signal to buy when the short crosses above the long average.
12. Parallel lines above and below the moving average line.
13. Each cycle is related to the next larger/shorter cycle by two.
14. Fibonacci series.
15. The moving average is placed days ahead of the actual price data.
16. The mean.

FILL-INS

1. The _____ _____ is used primarily as a trendfollowing device.

2. ___ ___ averages tend to be less sensitive to price action.

3. This type of indicator gives equal weight to each day's price. _____.

4. The _____ moving average is most often used when prices are in nontrending periods.

LESSON SEVEN 81

5. When employing two moving averages the _____ one is used for timing and the _____ one for identifying a trend.

6. In the triple crossover system the 4-day average will follow the trend most closely, followed by the 9-day and then the __-day.

7. One of the best known commodity market cycles is the _____ cycle.

8. Moving averages work best as indicators when the market is in a _____ period.

9. This breakout system is based on the dominant monthly cycle. _____.

10. When using a single moving average, _____ are often employed in order to minimize the occurrence of whipsaws.

MULTIPLE CHOICE

1. Short-term moving averages:
- **a.** Work better in sideways patterns.
- **b.** Generate more frequent false signals.
- **c.** Are precise.
- **d.** All of the above.

2. Which is one of the best known time cycles?
- **a.** Bimonthly cycle.
- **b.** 15-day cycle.
- **c.** Harmonic cycle.
- **d.** Monthly cycle.

3. Which statement is most accurate when closing prices move above the moving average?
- **a.** A buy signal is recommended.
- **b.** A hold signal is recommended.
- **c.** A sell signal is recommended.
- **d.** A sideways pattern will develop next.

4. The moving average is:
   a. Not a technical indicator.
   b. Subjective.
   c. A trendfollowing system.
   d. Largely ignored by technicians.
5. Fewer false signals will occur by:
   a. Using a lead time.
   b. Imposing filters.
   c. Using long moving averages.
   d. All of the above.

Refer to the following figure to answer question 6:

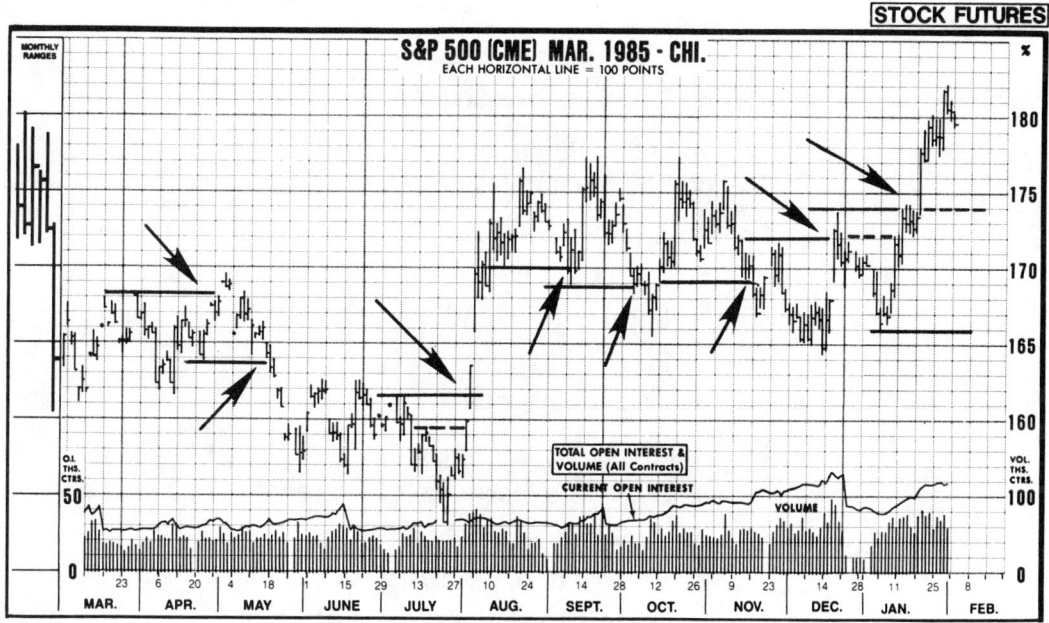

6. The period of September to January reveals:
   a. A sideways trading pattern.
   b. Frequent whipsaws.
   c. The difficulties associated with trendfollowing systems.
   d. All of the above.

7. When using a highlow band filter:
    a. The lower line in an uptrend resembles a bullish trendline.
    b. The upper line always intensifies whipsaw signals.
    c. A time filter is a necessity.
    d. The lower line is the line of defense for stoploss protection when the close is below the lower average.

8. The linear weighted moving average attempts to:
    a. Smooth out the moving average.
    b. Correct the weighting problem.
    c. Discount price action.
    d. Diminishes the weight given the most recent closing day.

9. What do cyclic analysts use most often to isolate underlying markets?
    a. The centering technique.
    b. The triple crossover method.
    c. Lead time.
    d. The reverse tally outcome system.

10. Moving averages are commonly applied to:
    a. Daily bar charts.
    b. Long range trend analysis.
    c. Point and figure charts.
    d. Logarithmic scales.

11. The exponentially smoothed moving average:
    a. Assigns a lesser weight to recent price action.
    b. Lacks sophistication.
    c. Discounts price data.
    d. Includes the entire price data of a specific futures contract.

12. "Envelopes" can be used to:
    a. Signify the onset of complex multiple units.
    b. Help reduce whipsaws.
    c. Retrace the entire previous move.
    d. Alert the technician of an impending trend reversal.

13. The system using the four preceding calendar weeks rule states:

    a. Cover long positions when prices fall.

    b. Liquidate long positions and sell short positions when prices fall.

    c. Liquidate short positions and cover long positions when prices rise.

    d. Cover short positions and liquidate long positions when prices rise.

Refer to the following figure to answer question 14:

LESSON SEVEN

14. The arrow to the solid line indicates:
   a. An example of a 4 week buy signal.
   b. A 4-11-28 combination.
   c. The linear weighted moving average.
   d. An example of optimization.

15. Another trend-following technique besides the moving average is:
   a. Weekly price channel.
   b. Rounding price channel.
   c. Line price channel.
   d. Exponential price channel.

16. Which statement(s) is/are true?
   a. Moving averages are trend predictors.
   b. Moving averages perform poorly in sideways markets.
   c. Moving averages are used rarely by technicians.
   d. None of the above.

17. In the triple crossover system which statement is most true?
   a. 4-11-28 is a popular combination.
   b. A buy alert occurs in an uptrend when day 4 crosses day 11 and 18.
   c. The 4 day average follows the trend the closest.
   d. All of the above.

18. When using two moving averages:
   a. The longer is used for timing.
   b. Both short and long averages are used for timing.
   c. The shorter average is for timing.
   d. None of the above.

Refer to the following figure to answer question 19:

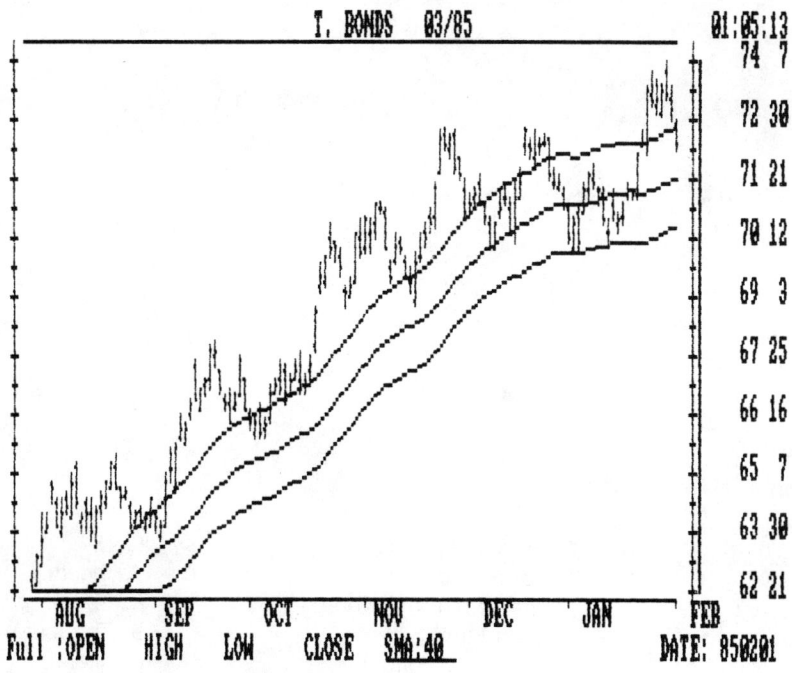

19. This is an example of:
   a. The use of a filter.
   b. The creation of a volatility band.
   c. Percentage envelopes.
   d. All of the above.

20. A sideline position is advised when:
   a. Prices are trending.
   b. Long averages are used for timing.
   c. Prices are between short and long averages.
   d. A triple crossover system is used.

Answer Sheet

MATCHING QUIZ

4	14
10	9
7	13
12	15
11	2
1	8
5	6

FILL-INS

1. moving average
2. Long-range
3. simple moving average
4. short-term
5. shorter . . . longer
6. 18-
7. monthly
8. trending
9. The four week rule
10. filters

MULTIPLE CHOICE

1. d As the answer implies, short-term moving averages work best in sideways patterns. Although they are more sensitive indicators than long moving averages, they also tend to give off more frequent false signals. Moving averages are not subjective but give precise signals.

2. d The best known cycle is the monthly cycle. Harmonic is a principle in cyclic analysis where each cycle is related to a shorter/longer cycle by two.

3. a As prices move above the moving average, a buy signal is advised. A sell signal is recommended when prices move below the moving average. There is no evidence to suggest that a sideways pattern will develop as a result of price moving above or below the moving average.

4. c The moving average is a trend-following technical indicator that is quite precise and widely used by technicians.

5. d When using lead time, a longer period is needed to penetrate the average which consequently results in fewer whipsaws. In addition, long averages are also conservative indicators that lessen the risk of false signals. Filters are always useful in helping to minimize false signals.

6. d This figure shows a sideways trading pattern during the months of September to January with frequent false signals given off; since all trend-following systems tend to miss market tops and bottoms, they are very useful but not perfect systems.

7. a Using a high-low band filter, the lower line acts as a bullish trendline in an uptrend. There is no evidence to support the upper line creating or intensifying the probability of whipsaws. Although filters are very useful, they are not always necessary. The upper line becomes the line of defense when there is a close below the lower line.

8. b The linear weighted moving average is designed to correct the weighting problem. The smoothed average occurs when using the exponentially smoothing average technique. The linear weighted approach gives greater weight to the more recent closing days.

9. a Centering is the statistically correct method for plotting averages and is preferred by cyclic analysts. The triple crossover method employs three different days of moving averages. Although lead time is used in placing averages, it is not the preferred method by cyclic analysts.

10. a Moving averages are most commonly applied to daily bar charts although they certainly could be used with long-term charts.

11. d The exponentially moving average does not discount price action. It is an exact technique—quite sophisticated—and assigns greater weight to the more recent action.

12. b This is the only possible correct answer since "envelopes" are filters. They do not retrace previous market moves nor do they predict trend reversal.

13. b The basic premise behind the four-week rule is to liquidate long position and sell short position when prices fall. Conversely, cover short positions and buy long when prices exceed the highs of the previous four calendar weeks.

14. a The arrow pointing to the solid line is a buy signal because of the four-week highs in the month of July. There is no 4-11-28 combination depicted on this chart. The linear moving average is not included on this chart. Optimization is a concept peculiar to specific markets in that each market has its own optimum moving average.

15. a Aside from moving averages, the weekly price channel or weekly rule, as it is commonly known, is another trend-following technique.

16. b Moving averages are trend-following; they are not market predictors of future trends. Moving averages are used frequently by technicians. Moving averages work best when markets are trending, and perform poorly in sideways markets.

17. c 4-11-28 is not a popular average. Since these combinations are not part of the triple crossover method, a buy alert does not occur when day four crosses days 11 and 28. The four-day average follows the trend most closely and would signal a buy alert if it crossed over days 9 and 18.

18. c The shorter average is for timing, and the larger average is used for trend identification.

19. d This figure shows how envelopes are used with moving averages. Envelopes are filters. Percentage envelopes are also known as volatility bands.

20. c A sidelines position is used primarily when prices are not trending. The triple crossover method is used when markets are trending. Long averages are used to identify trends.

LESSON EIGHT
Oscillators and Contrary Opinion

READING ASSIGNMENT

Chapter 10 of the text.

OBJECTIVES

- Understand how oscillators are used.
- Learn to identify divergences.
- Understand the contrary opinion method.
- Identify the characteristics of overbought and oversold market conditions.

READING ORIENTATION

This chapter is primarily about oscillators and how this technique is employed by technicians to determine overbought and oversold market conditions. The use of oscillators is another important technique available to the technicians that further enhances the analysts' ability to respond to market trends.

KEY TERMS

bullish consensus numbers, 317
contrary opinion, 316
danger zones, 282
divergence, 293
edge band analysis, 292
failure swings, 299
K% D, 304
MACDTM, 312
momentum, 277
normalized momentum line, 282
oscillator, 275
% R, 309
ROC, 284
RSI, 292
zero line, 281

Challenge

MATCHING QUIZ

____ oscillator
____ momentum
____ zero line
____ normalized momentum
____ ROC
____ edge band analysis
____ RSI
____ divergence
____ failure swings
____ K% D
____ % R
____ MACDTM
____ contrary opinion
____ bullish consensus numbers
____ danger zones

1. The opposite of majority agreement.
2. Oscillator and price line move in opposite directions.
3. Left/right conversion symbols.
4. A weekly indicator of market sentiment.
5. Vertical scale from 0 to 100.
6. The Stochastic Process.
7. Crossing of line generates buy & sell signals.
8. Aids in identifying overbought and oversold conditions.
9. Reading above 20 is overbought, below 80 is oversold.
10. Identification of boundary extremes.
11. Measures the velocity of prices.
12. Warn of extreme overbought or oversold conditions.
13. The RSI is above 70 or below 30 before reversing.
14. An oscillator using two exponential moving averages.
15. The line falls within a +1 or −1 range.
16. Rate of change.

LESSON EIGHT

FILL-INS

1. In conjunction with price charts, _____ can identify short-term market extremes.

2. As a rule, crossing the _____ usually signals important trading signals.

3. The measurement of _____ requires the taking of price differences for a fixed time interval.

4. The momentum indicator measures the rate of _____ or _____.

5. The RSI uses a vertical scale when movement above __ is overbought and a move below __ is oversold.

6. When a double top or bottom is formed on an oscillator, possible _____ exists.

7. Two lines are used in the stochastic process—____ line and the ____ line.

8. Using price ratios is one method to measure the ____.

9. _____ _____ assesses the degree of bullishness or bearishness among speculators.

10. When using Bullish Consensus numbers, a change in trend direction by __ is usually significant.

11. Oscillators are especially valuable toward the ____ of market moves.

12. The _____ ____ leads the advance or decline of the price movement by a few days.

MULTIPLE CHOICE

Please refer to the following figure to answer question 1:

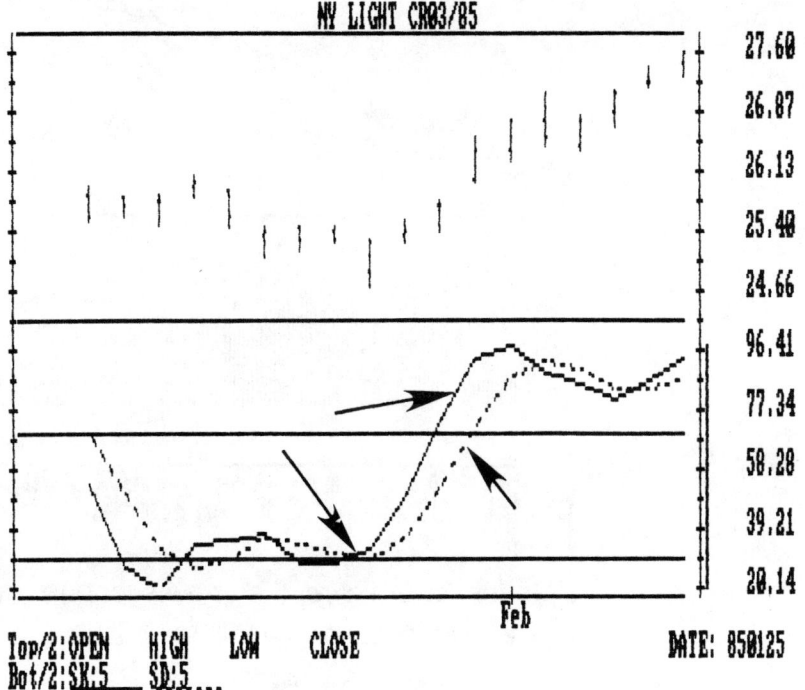

1. In this figure of stochastics, the upper arrow is:
    a. % K.
    b. ROC.
    c. % D.
    d. MACDTM.

Refer to the following figure to answer question 2:

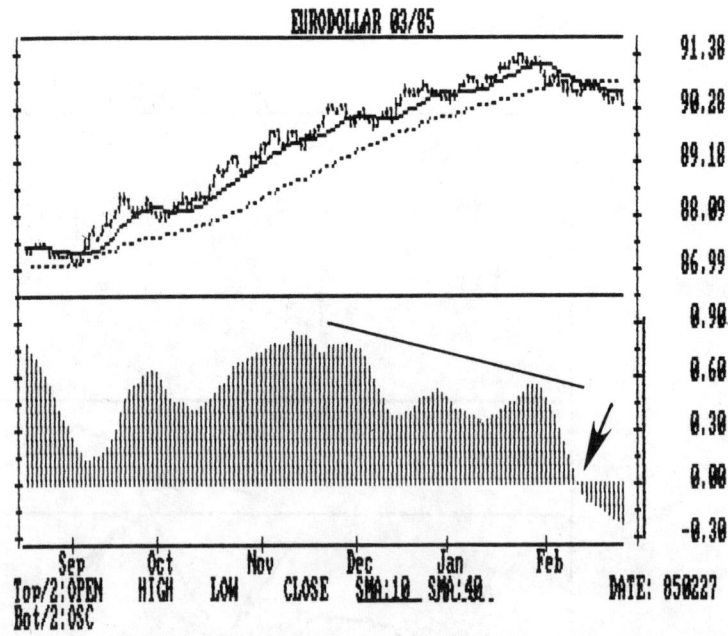

2. In the lower figure, the arrow supports:
    a. The need for time filters.
    b. A major buy signal.
    c. A major sell signal.
    d. None of the above.
3. Oscillators are most useful when:
    a. Its value is at extreme boundaries.
    b. There is divergence.
    c. The zero line is crossed.
    d. All of the above.
4. Which statement is most accurate?
    a. Momentum charts lack a zero line.
    b. Crossing above the zero line is used as a trading signal.
    c. A cross above the zero line is a sell signal.
    d. A cross below the zero line is a buy signal.

5. When two moving averages are too far apart:
    a. A downtrend is likely.
    b. The trend will probably not stall.
    c. A market extreme is created.
    d. Oscillators will provide little new information.
6. The RSI resolves the problem of:
    a. Erratic movement caused by sharp price changes.
    b. Equalization.
    c. Needing upper and lower boundary ranges.
    d. None of the above.
7. The 70 and 30 lines are often used to:
    a. Form the % R oscillator.
    b. Establish the beginning of non-trending patterns.
    c. Generate signals.
    d. All of the above.
8. In the stochastic process, the:
    a. % D line is of secondary importance to the % K line.
    b. % R line is a minor trend indicator.
    c. % K line is irrelevant.
    d. % D line is more important in signalling major trends.
9. A simple way to use the oscillator is to:
    a. Use a bi-normal measuring system.
    b. Use stochastics.
    c. Measure the rate of change.
    d. Establish the zero line as a signal indicator.
10. Which of the following are used for oscillator interpretation?
    I. The crossing of the zero line.
    II. Edge Band Analysis.
    III. Divergence.
    a. I only.
    b. I and II only.
    c. II and III only.
    d. All of the above.

11. The most widely followed oscillator is the:
   a. ROC.
   b. RSI.
   c. MACDTM.
   d. K% D.

12. In general, analysts stress that:
   a. Oscillators are not frequently used to time market entry.
   b. Oscillators are of little use during trending periods.
   c. Oscillator buy signals must be confirmed by divergence analysis.
   d. Oscillator buy signals work best in uptrends.

13. Which statement is most accurate?
   a. Peaks and troughs on a price chart coincide with peaks and troughs on the oscillator in choppy markets.
   b. Oscillators are poor monitors of sideways price movement.
   c. Greater attention to oscillators is necessary in the early stages of a move.
   d. Oscillators tend to give off frequent false signals as the move reaches maturity.

14. A true contrarian:
   a. Has little use for the technical analysis approach.
   b. Follows the fundamental analyst's philosophy.
   c. Will act in the opposite direction of the majority.
   d. All of the above.

15. In the stochastic process, the best buy signals occur when the:
   a. D value is in the 10–15 range.
   b. K value is in the 25–30 range.
   c. R value is negated by D and K.
   d. D value is above the zero line.

16. When two declining peaks are formed as prices continue to move higher, a bearish divergence occurs when the:
   a. K line is above 70.
   b. D line is above 70.
   c. D line is below 70.
   d. D line is below 30.

17. In Williams % R:
  a. An overbought reading is below 20.
  b. An oversold reading is above 80.
  c. A time period of ¼ cycle length is used.
  d. None of the above.

18. In using ROC, if the latest price is higher than the price 10 days ago:
  a. The ratio would be between +1 and −1.
  b. The ratio would be above 100.
  c. The ratio would be below 100.
  d. The ratio would hold at a constant until the market changed trends.

19. When using the Current Relative Strength (CRS) oscillator during the bull-market corrections:
  a. The CRS line stays at the 70 line.
  b. The CRS line crosses the zero line.
  c. The CRS line moves sideways.
  d. The CRS line usually declines to and bounces off the zero line.

20. An important requirement for divergence analysis is that the:
  a. Divergence must incorporate the principle of stochastics.
  b. Divergence must be temporary.
  c. Divergence occurs near oscillator extremes.
  d. All of the above.

Answer Sheet

MATCHING QUIZ

8	13
11	6
7	9
15	14
16	1
10	4
5	12
2	

FILL-INS

1. oscillators
2. zero line
3. market momentum
4. ascent . . . descent
5. RSI . . . 70 . . . 30
6. divergence
7. % K line . . . % D line
8. ROC
9. Contrary opinion
10. 5%
11. end
12. momentum line

MULTIPLE CHOICE

1. a This figure is an example of stochastics. The upper arrow is % K and the dashed arrow is % D. "ROC" stands for rate of change, and "MACDTM" is the Moving Average Convergence/Divergence Trading Method.

2. c In this figure the arrow points to an area that shows the oscillator crossing below the zero line. Therefore, a major sell signal is indicated since the oscillator moved below the zero line. Although time filters are useful, they are not relevant to this question.

3. d Choices a, b, and c are the three most important uses for the oscillator. The described situations are common to most oscillators.

4. b In its most simple form, the crossing of the zero line is used as a trading signal. Momentum charts have zero lines. Answers c and d are confusing in that a cross above the zero line is a buy signal and a cross below, a sell signal.

5. c As the moving averages move farther apart, market extremes are created. Oscillators are important data sources. However, it is presumptuous to say that a downtrend with occur or that the trend will not stall.

6. a The Relative Strength Index (RSI) solves the problem of erratic movement caused by sharp price changes. Boundary lines are also part of the RSI.

7. c The 70/30 lines are used to generate buy/sell signals. They are not intended to establish nontrending patterns since market conditions dictate such patterns.

8. d In the stochastic process, the % D line is of primary importance; the % K line is secondary. The % R oscillator differs somewhat from the stochastic process.

9. d The simplest way to use oscillators is to establish the zero line as a signal indicator. Binominal systems are not relevant to oscillators. Stochastics are complicated although quite useful. The rate of change is a ratio construct which again is useful though not necessarily simple.

10. d When interpreting oscillators, statements I, II, and III are commonly used. Although the other choices are correct, d is the most accurate and comprehensive answer.

11. b Technicians most often employ the RSI. Although the other techniques are also used, the RSI is the most widely followed.

12. d Analysts stress that oscillator buy signals work best in uptrends. Oscillators can be used to time market entry. Oscillators are, of course, quite useful during trending periods. Although divergence analysis is important, it is not necessary to generate buy signals.

13. a Choice "a" is the most accurate statement. Oscillators provide important information during sideways markets. Oscillators work best when the move has matured, not when it first begins.

14. c A true contrarian acts in the opposite direction of the majority. Although they are grouped under the technical analysis approach, they tend to utilize a psychological analysis approach to market moves.

15. a Apparently, the D value range of 10–15 is the best buy signal. Remember that the D *not* K value is the more important and the one used for trading signals (% R) is not part of the stochastic process.

16. b Answer B is correct. When the D line is below 30, a bullish divergence is possible.

17. d In Williams % R, an overbought reading is above 20. An oversold reading is under 80. The time period is ½ the cycle length.

18. b "The ratio is above 100" is the correct response. +1 and −1 designations are not used in the ROC. Zero as a constant is not used in this system.

19. d In general, the CRS lines tend to decline to and then bounce off the zero line during bull market corrections. This is the general rule; therefore, the CRS line would not stay at 70, cross below the zero line, or move sideways.

20. c This is a basic point to remember about oscillators—divergence occurs near oscillator extremes. Stochastics and divergence are not interdependent on each other. "Divergence must be temporary" is not supported in the readings.

LESSON NINE

Point and Figure Charting

READING ASSIGNMENT

    Chapters 11 and 12 of the text.

OBJECTIVES

- Identify point and figure charts.
- Develop a basic understanding of how to plot point and figure charts.
- Understand the various uses of point and figure charts.

READING ORIENTATION

    These two chapters depart from the discussion of bar charts. Depending on the type of trading, a point and figure chart can be used as another valuable technical indicator. Samples are provided to help the reader develop a "feel" for plotting, It will quickly become obvious that this sample technique is easy to learn and can provide the technician with important trading information.

KEY TERMS

bearish support line, 357
box size, 329
catapult, 341
channel lines, 360
congestion area, 336
45-degree angle, 356
fulcrum, 339
horizontal count, 338
intra-day point and figure chart, 342
O column, 325
one-point reversal chart, 334
point and figure chart, 324
pyramiding, 363
reversal criterion, 329
sell signal, 352
three-point reversal chart, 351
Victor de Villiers, 322
X column, 325

Challenge

MATCHING QUIZ

___5___ O column
_____ point & figure charts
_____ fulcrum
_____ congestion area
_____ intra-day point and figure chart
_____ pyramiding
_____ X column
_____ one-point reversal chart
_____ sell signal
_____ reversal criterion
_____ horizontal count
_____ catapult
_____ box size
_____ channel lines

1. Value assigned to each box on a chart.
2. Xs and Os are present in the same column.
3. Time reference points.
4. The width of the pattern.
5. Represents declining prices.
6. A retracement of boxes necessary to cause a reversal.
7. Study of pure price movement.
8. A column of Os decline one box below the lowest O in the prior column.
9. Used primarily as timing aids.
10. Vertical measurements to obtain price objectives.
11. A congestion area that forms an accumulation base or distribution top.
12. Adding additional positions as the market moves in the right direction.
13. Point and figure charting.
14. Sideways price movement with well-defined tops/bottoms.
15. A breakout.
16. Widely used by floor traders.
17. Represents rising prices.
18. When the channel line is in an uptrend.
19. Only the high and low prices are plotted for the day.

FILL-INS

1. The _____ ___ helps determine in advance the direction of the breakout.

2. The ___ ___ ___ ___ doesn't take time into consideration as the price action is plotted.

3. Trading signals are more/less precise on point and figure charts than on bar charts.

4. When using modified (not intra-day) three point reversal charts, Xs and Os should ____ be drawn on the same day.

5. _____ is not included on point and figure charts.

6. Point and figure charts provide the technician with specific ____ and ____ points.

7. A market condition where no three-box reversals occur during a trend is called a ____.

8. ____ _____ ____ can be used in order to keep track of calendar time.

9. The most important value of point and figure charts is the ability of the technician to identify _____ and _____ zones.

10. The _____ ____ ____ ____ ____ technique is most useful for very short-term trading.

MULTIPLE CHOICE

Refer to the following charts to answer questions 1 and 2:

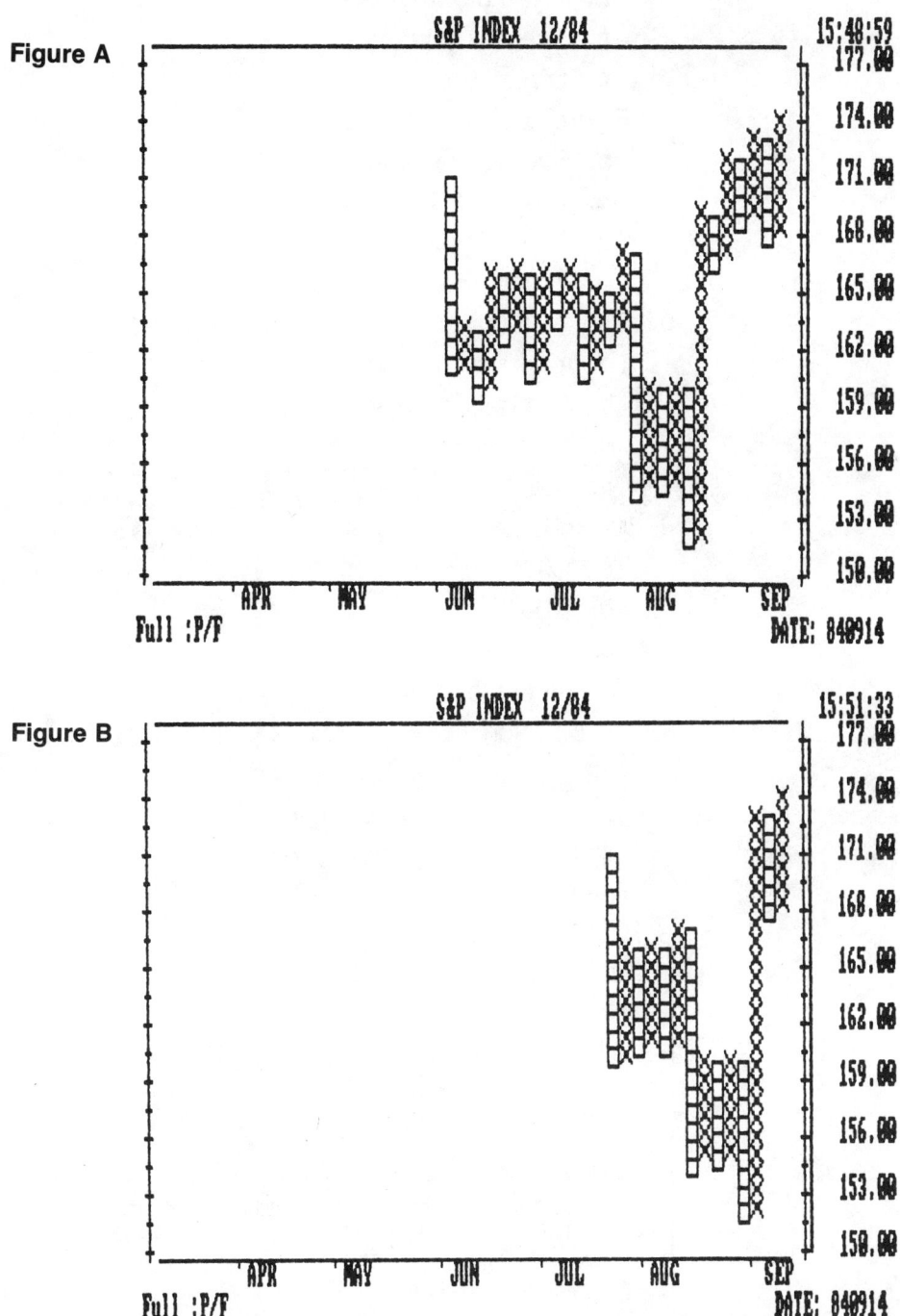

Figure A

Figure B

1. Figure A is an example of a:
   a. Five-box reversal.
   b. Three-box reversal.
   c. One-box reversal.
   d. Triple Top.
2. Figure B is an example of a:
   a. Five-box reversal.
   b. Three-box reversal.
   c. One-box reversal.
   d. Profits and profitability chart.
3. Point and figure charts can be made more sensitive by using:
   a. A smaller reversal number.
   b. A larger reversal number.
   c. Time reference points.
   d. The X column.
4. Which is an example of a box size value?
   a. 1.00
   b. 2.00
   c. 5.00
   d. All of the above.
5. The traditional order of reversal criteria is:
   a. Three-one-five box reversal.
   b. One-two-three box reversal.
   c. One-three-five box reversal.
   d. Five-three-one box reversal.

Refer to the following figure to answer question 6:

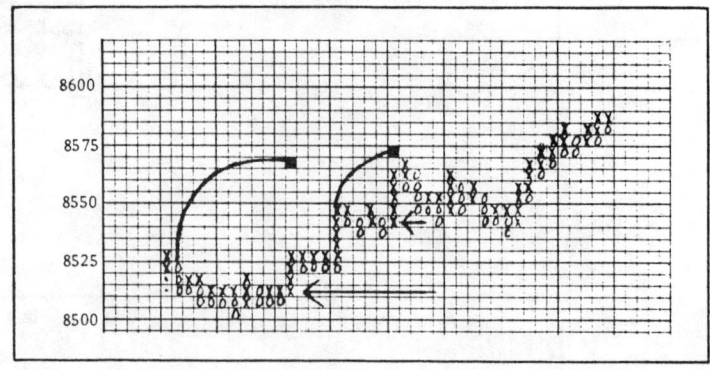

6. This figure depicts:
   a. A one-day cycle.
   b. The problems that congestion areas produce.
   c. Long-term plotting.
   d. How price objectives are determined.

Please refer to the following figure to answer question 7:

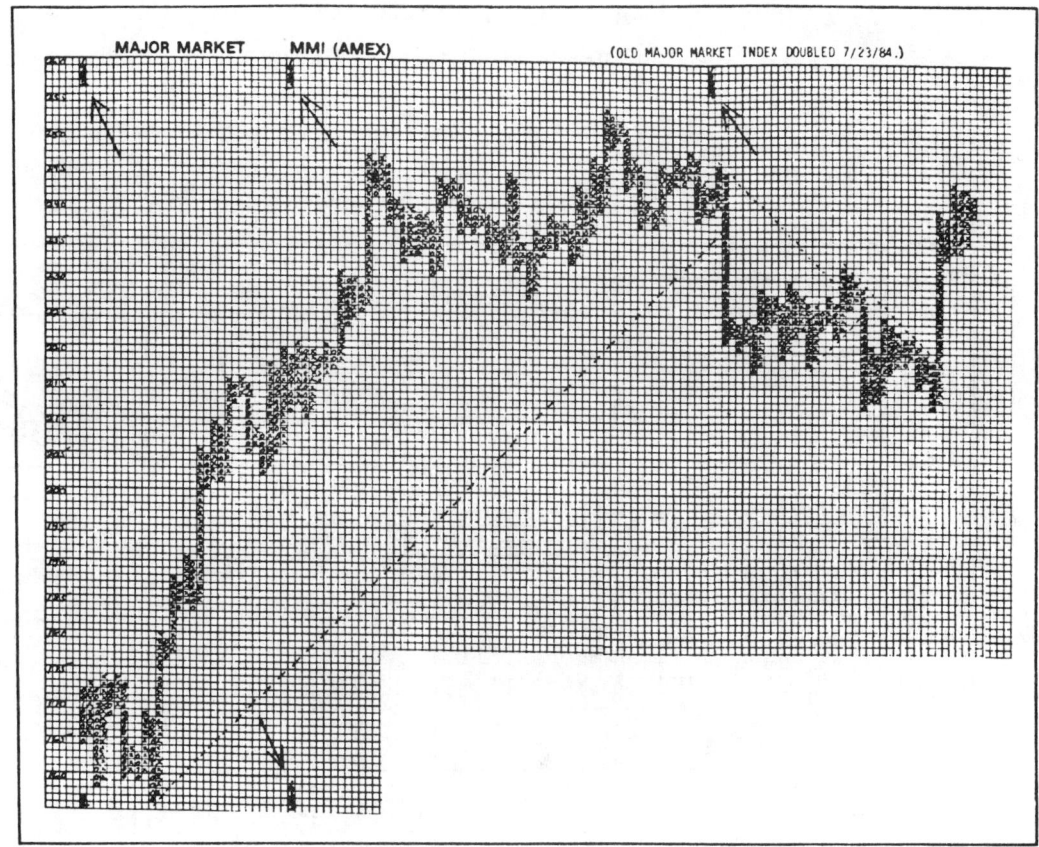

7. The dashed line indicates:
   a. Trendlines always connecting tops and bottoms.
   b. A 45-degree trendline.
   c. An intra-day chart.
   d. The conventional use of drawing trendlines.

8. When using point and figure charts:
   a. A trendline can be used as a filter.
   b. Short positions are covered on any simple buy signal.
   c. Long positions are liquidated on any simple sell signal.
   d. All of the above.

9. Point and figure charts are ideal in that:
   a. There is only one single box and reversal size.
   b. They have one specific use.
   c. Generalized entry and exit points are sometimes obtainable.
   d. Trading signals are more precise than on bar charts.

Refer to the following figure to answer question 10:

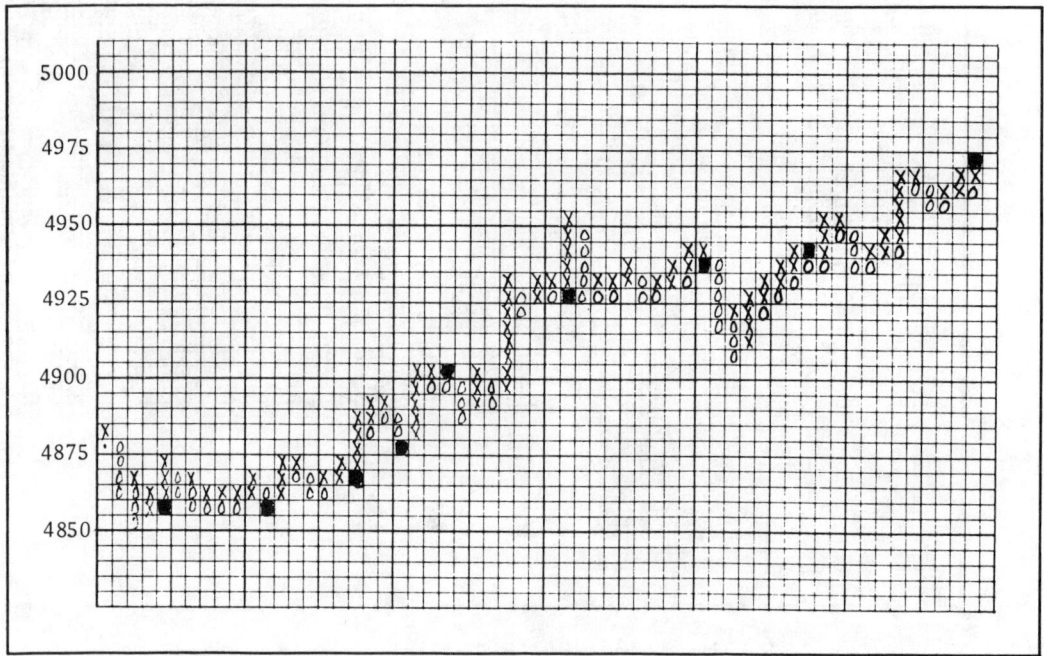

10. In this figure, which statement is most accurate?
   a. The use of Xs and Os in the same column never occurs.
   b. This is an example of a three-box reversal.
   c. The blackened boxes are used as reference points.
   d. None of the above.

11. In obtaining price objectives for point and figure charts:
   a. The horizontal count is the method used the most.
   b. Vertical measurements are used most often.
   c. The statistical method using the R coefficient is employed.
   d. Price objectives cannot be obtained on point and figure charts.

12. A fulcrum:
   a. Is a congestion area.
   b. Occurs after a significant advance or decline.
   c. Forms an accumulation base or distribution top.
   d. All of the above.

Please refer to the following figure to answer question 13:

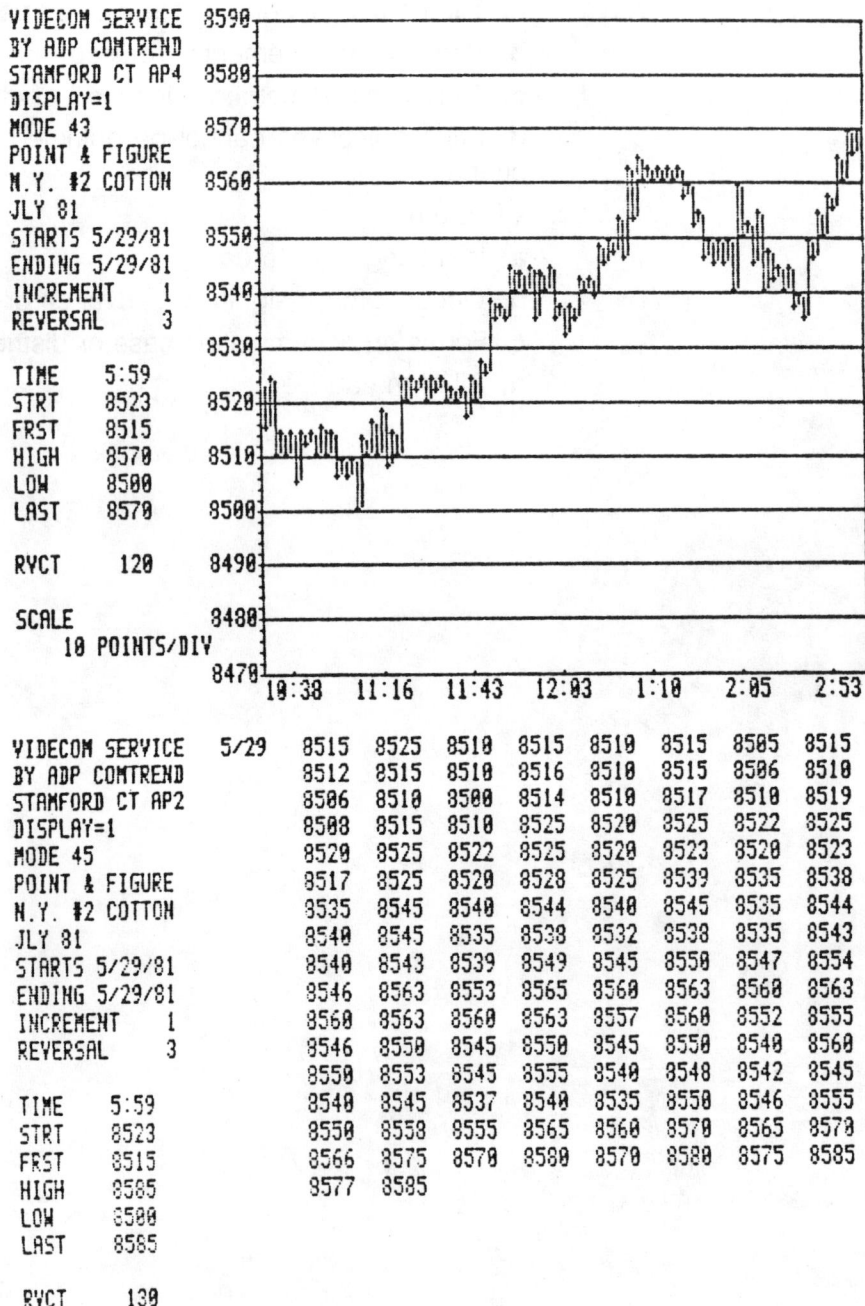

13. The listed numbers below the figure are:
   a. Primarily selling codes.
   b. Computerized codes used for plotting purposes.
   c. Used to plot point and figure charts.
   d. Primarily buying codes.

14. Point and figure charts are designed to measure:
   a. Time and price movement.
   b. Time movement.
   c. Price movement.
   d. Time, price, and breadth movement.

15. A difficulty associated with trading primarily on simple signals is the:
   a. Rarity of such signals.
   b. Frequency of these signals.
   c. Complex quality of these signals.
   d. Lack of profitability with this system.

Answer Sheet

MATCHING QUIZ

5	2
7	8
11	6
14	4
16	15
12	1
17	9

FILL-INS

1. congestion area
2. point and figure chart
3. more
4. never
5. Volume
6. entry . . . exit
7. pole
8. Time reference points
9. support . . . resistance
10. intra-day point and figure chart

MULTIPLE CHOICE

1. b This is an example of a three-box reversal. Figure A is a one-box reversal. Figure C is a five-box reversal. There is no indication of a triple top formation.

2. b This is an example of a five-box reversal employing the point and figure method of charting.

3. a Sensitivity occurs by smaller reversal numbers. Reference points are selected by the user. They are not part of determining price movements in point and figure charts. The X column is used for plotting purposes.

4. d All of the listed values can be used to determine box sizes. The larger the box value, the less sensitive the chart.

5. c Traditionally, the order used is to begin with the one-box reversal chart and then move to the three- and five-box reversal.

6. d This figure demonstrates how price objectives are determined. The analyst counts the number of columns across the horizontal congestion area in order to determine price objectives.

7. b The dashed line in this figure depicts a 45-degree trendline. It is used only on the three-box reversal charts. It is not a conventional way to draw trendlines. Because of the severe condensation on these charts, it's impractical to connect tops and bottoms.

8. d Trendlines are used as filters on point and figure charts. Choices b and c are true—short positions are covered on a simple buy signal.

9. d Because of their design, point and figure charts are much more precise than bar charts in terms of trading signals. Box and reversal sizes can and do vary. There are many different ways these charts are used for entry and exit points. Entry and exit points are also specific on these charts.

10. c This figure is a one-box reversal chart which allows Xs and Os to occupy the same column. The blackened boxed identify the end of each day's trading.

11. a When obtaining price objectives, the horizontal count is most often used. The vertical measure is used less frequently. There is no statistical R coefficient used to determine the price objective for point and figure charts.

12. d The term "fulcrum" (or "congestion area") includes in its definition all of the listed choices. This is a fairly common occurrence in point and figure charting.

13. c The listed numbers in this figure are the data necessary to construct point and figure charts. In this figure, the Xs and Os have been replaced by arrows.

14. c Point and figure charts are meant to record pure price movement and not time. In fact, these charts ignore time.

15. b When trading only or primarily on simple signals, the analyst can spend a considerable amount of money because the simple signals recur so frequently. They are, however, more apt to point to profitable opportunities.

Final Examination

Questions 1-5 refer to FIGURE 1:

1. The breakout at point a above the peak at point 2 initiated an uptrend / downtrend / neutral trend (circle one).

2. The "sell signal" at point b broke the major up trendline. The up trendline should be drawn below points _____ and _____ (fill in the blanks).

3. The selloff from points 8 to 9 shows three downside gaps. The downside gap at b is a breakaway / measuring / exhaustion gap?

4. The two peaks at 6 and 8 show a _____ _____ reversal pattern.

5. The bottom at point 9 shows a gap on either side. This type of gap pattern is called an _____ _____.

FIGURE 1

FINAL EXAMINATION

Questions 6–10 refer to FIGURE 2:

6. During the uptrend, the downside correction from point 5 to 6 most resembles a flag / pennant?

7. The breakdown at point 12 appears to complete a _____ _____ reversal pattern.

8. Assuming the height of the topping pattern (the vertical distance between points 9 and 10) is about $25, the minimum downside target from the sell signal at $420 measures to $_____.

9. Just prior to the first peak (at point 9), a gap shows up prominently. This is a breakaway / measuring / exhaustion gap.

10. After support at $400 was broken on the downside, a down trendline should have been drawn connecting which two peaks? 11 / 13 / 15 (circle two).

FIGURE 2

FINAL EXAMINATION

Questions 11–15 refer to FIGURE 3:

11. The major up trendline should be drawn below points _____ and _____.

12. The intermediate decline from point 2 to 3 is an example of a 33% / 50% / 67% retracement?

13. The sideways price pattern following the peak at 4 can best be described as a _____.

14. That type of pattern described in the previous question is usually a reversal / continuation pattern.

15. If the trend were to turn downward, the previous peak at point 2 would now function as a support / resistance level.

FIGURE 3

FINAL EXAMINATION

Questions 16–20 refer to FIGURE 4:

16. During the initial rally, three gaps are shown at points a, b, and c. The middle gap at point b is a breakaway / measuring / exhaustion gap.

17. Of the three "gap" types, the filling of the _____ gap is most often a warning that a turn in the trend is near.

18. The large formation, from points 2 to 6, most resembles a _____ triangle.

19. In this case, that type of pattern would normally signal higher / lower prices.

20. The upside measurement from this type of pattern is usually the width / height of the pattern?

FIGURE 4

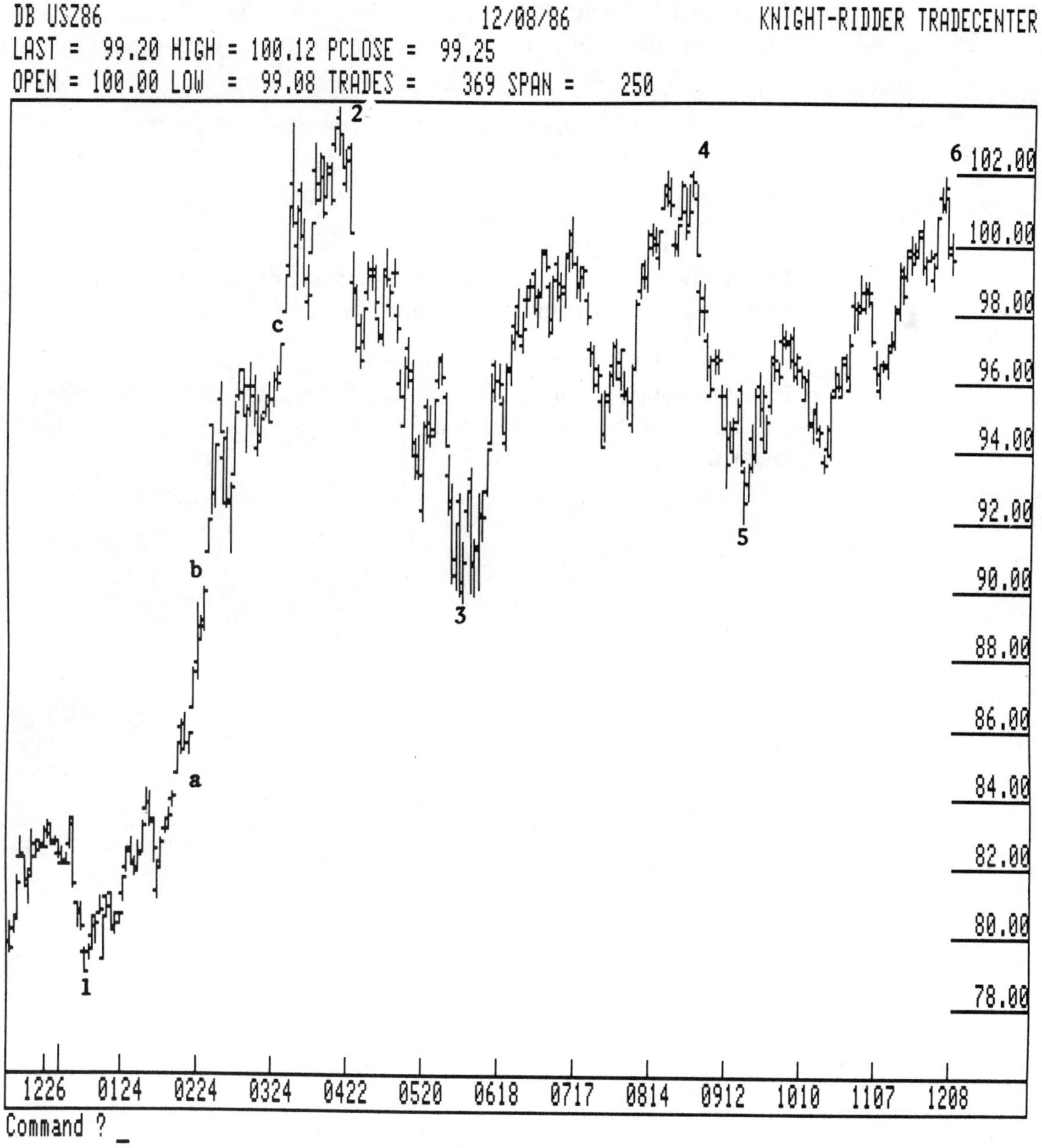
DB USZ86
12/08/86
KNIGHT-RIDDER TRADECENTER
LAST = 99.20 HIGH = 100.12 PCLOSE = 99.25
OPEN = 100.00 LOW = 99.08 TRADES = 369 SPAN = 250
1
a
b
c
2
3
4
5
6
102.00
100.00
98.00
96.00
94.00
92.00
90.00
88.00
86.00
84.00
82.00
80.00
78.00
1226
0124
0224
0324
0422
0520
0618
0717
0814
0912
1010
1107
1208
Command ? _

Questions 21–25 refer to FIGURE 5:

21. About halfway through the upleg 1-2, a small consolidation pattern is visible at point a. That pattern most closely resembles a _____.

22. That type of pattern (at point a) rarely lasts more than 1 / 3 / 5 weeks in an uptrend.

23. During the subsequent decline from point 2 to 3, the price formation (b, c, d, e, f, g) resembles a _____ _____.

24. Assuming the height of the previous consolidation pattern is $100, and the breakdown point (h) is at $560, the minimum downside target would be to $_____.

25. A small gap appears just above the recent action (at point i). The ability of prices to move above the gap would signal higher / lower prices.

FIGURE 5

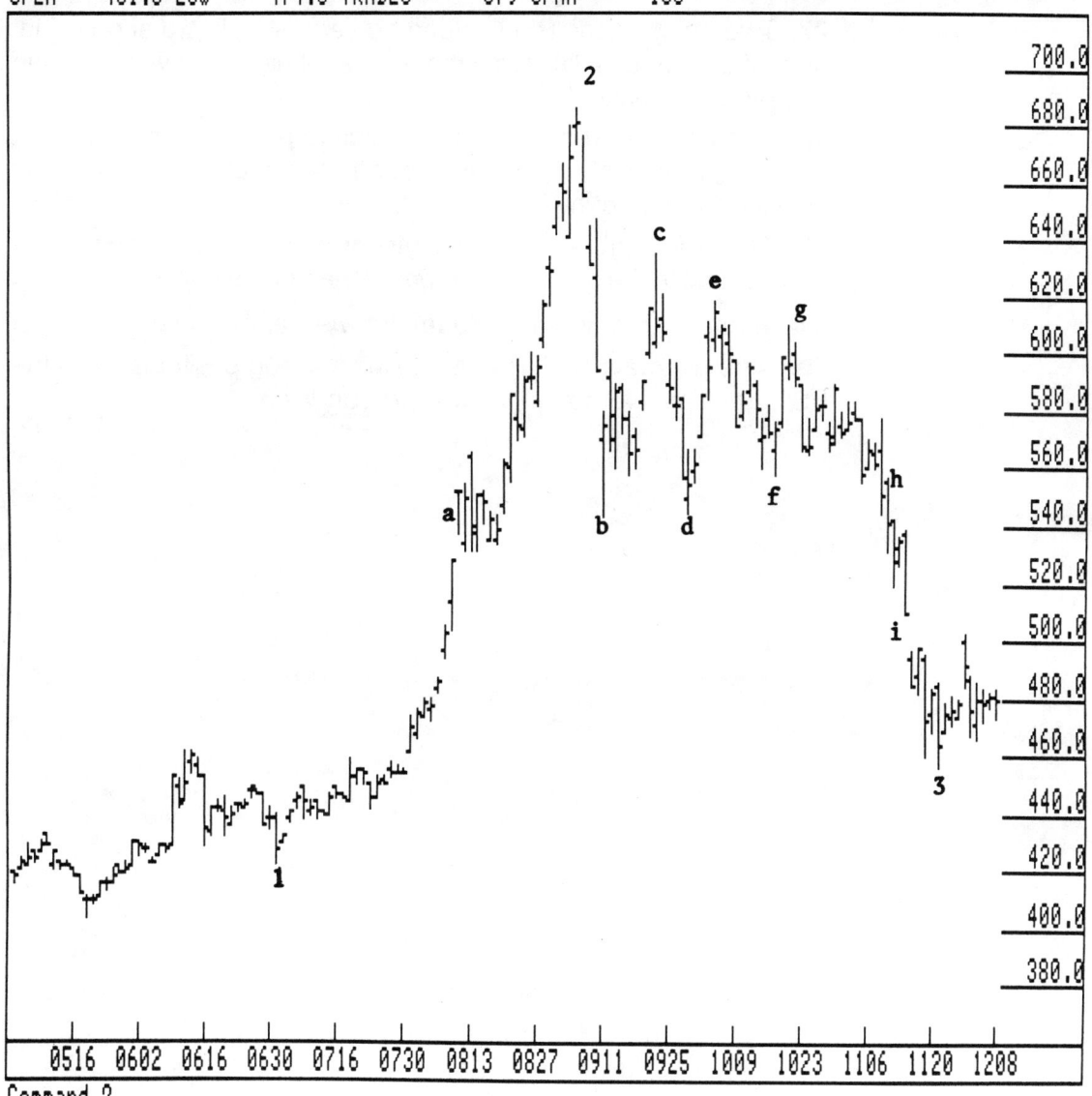

FINAL EXAMINATION

127

Questions 26–30 refer to FIGURE 6:

26. The chart along the bottom of this figure is the RSI line, which is used as an oscillator. At this point, the RSI line is overbought / oversold / neutral.

27. Two peaks in the RSI line can be seen at points a and b. That type of pattern usually warns the analyst of higher / lower prices in that type of situation.

28. Two troughs are seen in the RSI line at points c and d at about the same level. Given the market conditions, that type of formation is usually a sign of higher / lower prices.

29. At present, prices are in a neutral trading range. If prices were to break out to the upside, what would the upside target be utilizing the "measured move" technique? Answer: approximately _____.

30. As a general rule, it is better to initiate long positions when the RSI line is an overbought / oversold condition.

FIGURE 6

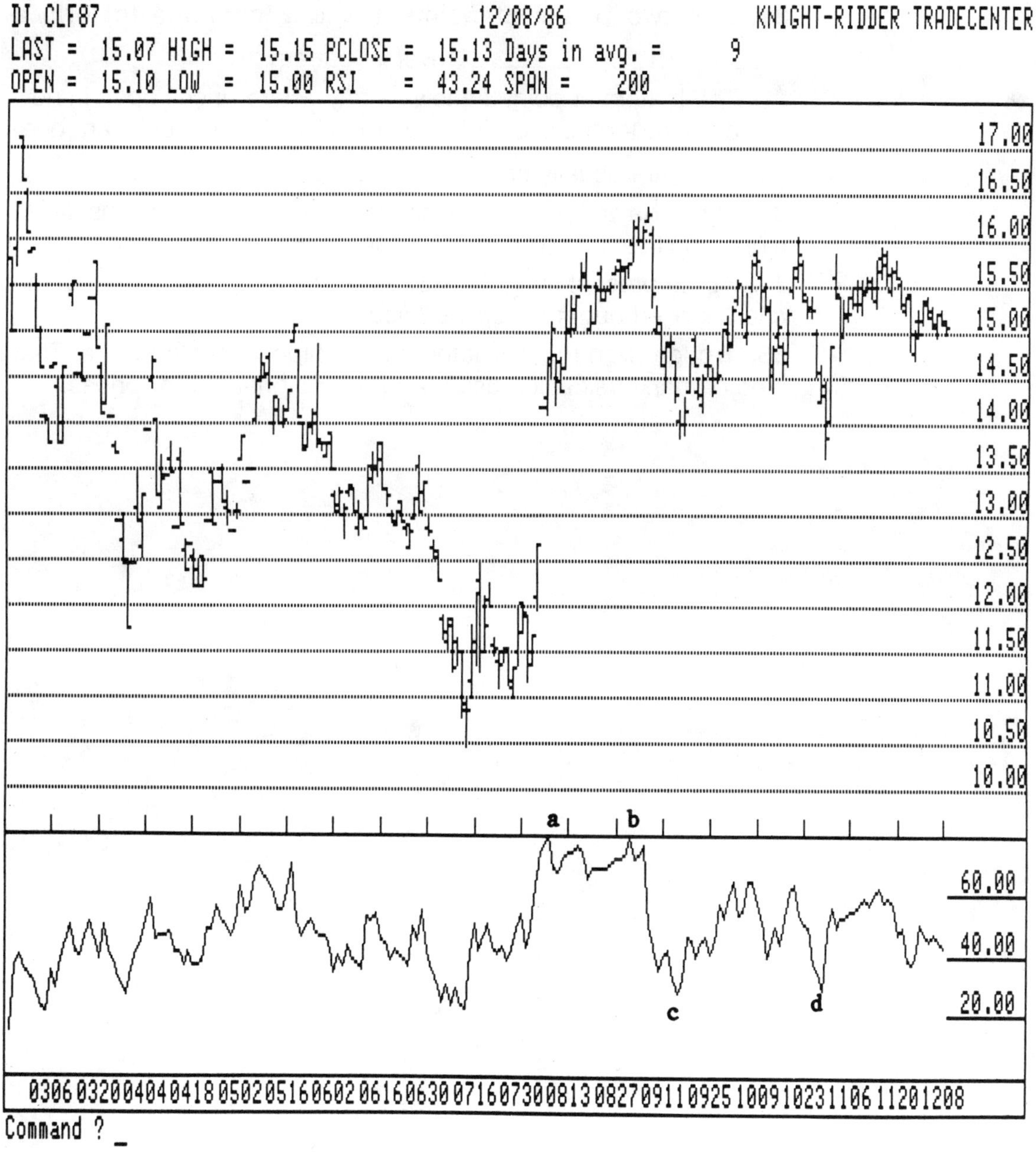
DI CLF87 12/08/86 KNIGHT-RIDDER TRADECENTER
LAST = 15.07 HIGH = 15.15 PCLOSE = 15.13 Days in avg. = 9
OPEN = 15.10 LOW = 15.00 RSI = 43.24 SPAN = 200
17.00
16.50
16.00
15.50
15.00
14.50
14.00
13.50
13.00
12.50
12.00
11.50
11.00
10.50
10.00
a
b
60.00
40.00
20.00
c
d
0306 0320 0404 0418 0502 0516 0602 0616 0630 0716 0730 0813 0827 0911 0925 1009 1023 1106 1120 1208
Command ? _

Questions 31–36 refer to FIGURE 7:

31. The two peaks at points 1 and 2 combine to form a _____ _____ reversal pattern.

32. The bottom at point 3 shows a day where prices open in new low ground, then close higher on the day. These significant one-day turns are usually called _____ _____ _____.

33. These days described in the previous question are considered more significant if volume for the day is heavier / lighter.

34. At the present time, the RSI oscillator along the bottom of the chart is overbought / oversold / neutral.

35. Trough b on the oscillator chart is higher than trough a. That type of market situation usually calls for higher / lower prices.

FIGURE 7

FINAL EXAMINATION

Questions 36–40 refer to FIGURE 8:

36. The two lines along the bottom of the chart are part of the stochastic oscillator formulation. Over the past week, the oscillator has just given a short-term "buy" / "sell" signal.

37. The major up trendline on such a chart should connect which two points? _____ and _____.

38. A buying situation is usually indicated when the dotted (K line) is above / under the solid (D line).

39. A selling situation is usually indicated when the dotted (K line) is above / under the solid (D line).

40. The buy or sell signal is considered stronger / weaker if both lines are moving in the same direction at the time of the crossover. (Circle either "stronger" or "weaker.")

FIGURE 8

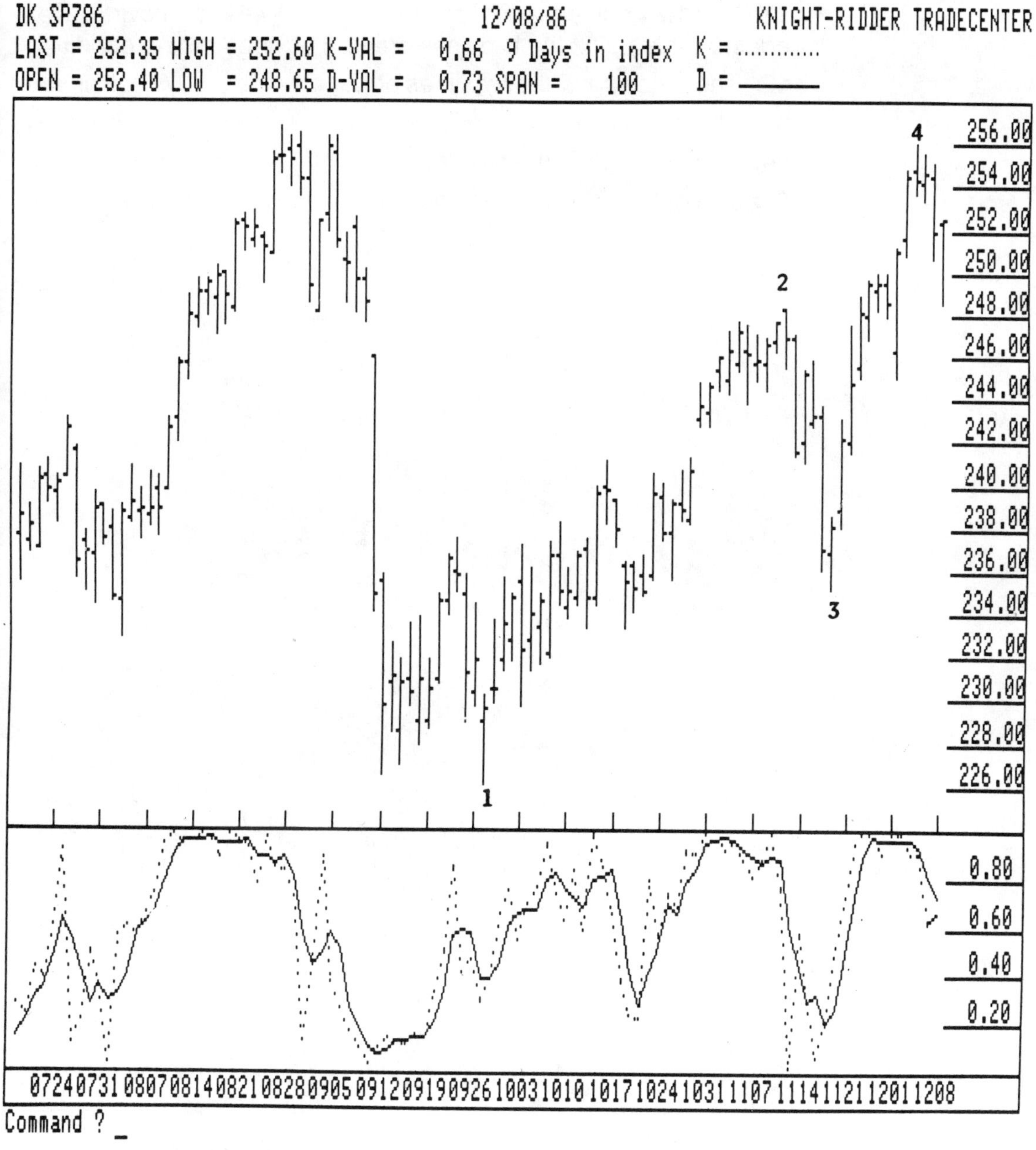
DK SPZ86
12/08/86
KNIGHT-RIDDER TRADECENTER
LAST = 252.35 HIGH = 252.60 K-VAL = 0.66 9 Days in index K = ...
OPEN = 252.40 LOW = 248.65 D-VAL = 0.73 SPAN = 100 D = ______
256.00
254.00
252.00
250.00
248.00
246.00
244.00
242.00
240.00
238.00
236.00
234.00
232.00
230.00
228.00
226.00
1
2
3
4
0.80
0.60
0.40
0.20
0724 0731 0807 0814 0821 0828 0905 0912 0919 0926 1003 1010 1017 1024 1031 1107 1114 1121 1201 1208
Command ? _

Questions 41–45 refer to FIGURE 9:

41. The two curving lines are the 10- and 40-day moving averages. At this point, the two lines are in a buying / selling condition.

42. The crossing of the two lines at point 1 was a buy / sell signal.

43. The crossing of the two lines at point 2 was a buy / sell signal.

44. The crossing of the two lines at point 3 was a buy / sell signal.

45. The crossing of the two lines at point 4 was a buy / sell signal.

FIGURE 9

FINAL EXAMINATION

Questions 46–50 refer to FIGURE 10:

46. The two moving average lines are 5 and 20 days. Using shorter moving average lines produces more / fewer signals.

47. Using shorter moving average lines produces faster / slower signals.

48. The moving average crossing at point 1 gave a buy / sell signal.

49. At present, the moving average alignment is bullish / bearish.

50. The fact that the two lines are fairly wide apart at the moment suggests that the downtrend will probably accelerate / consolidate.

END OF EXAMINATION

FIGURE 10

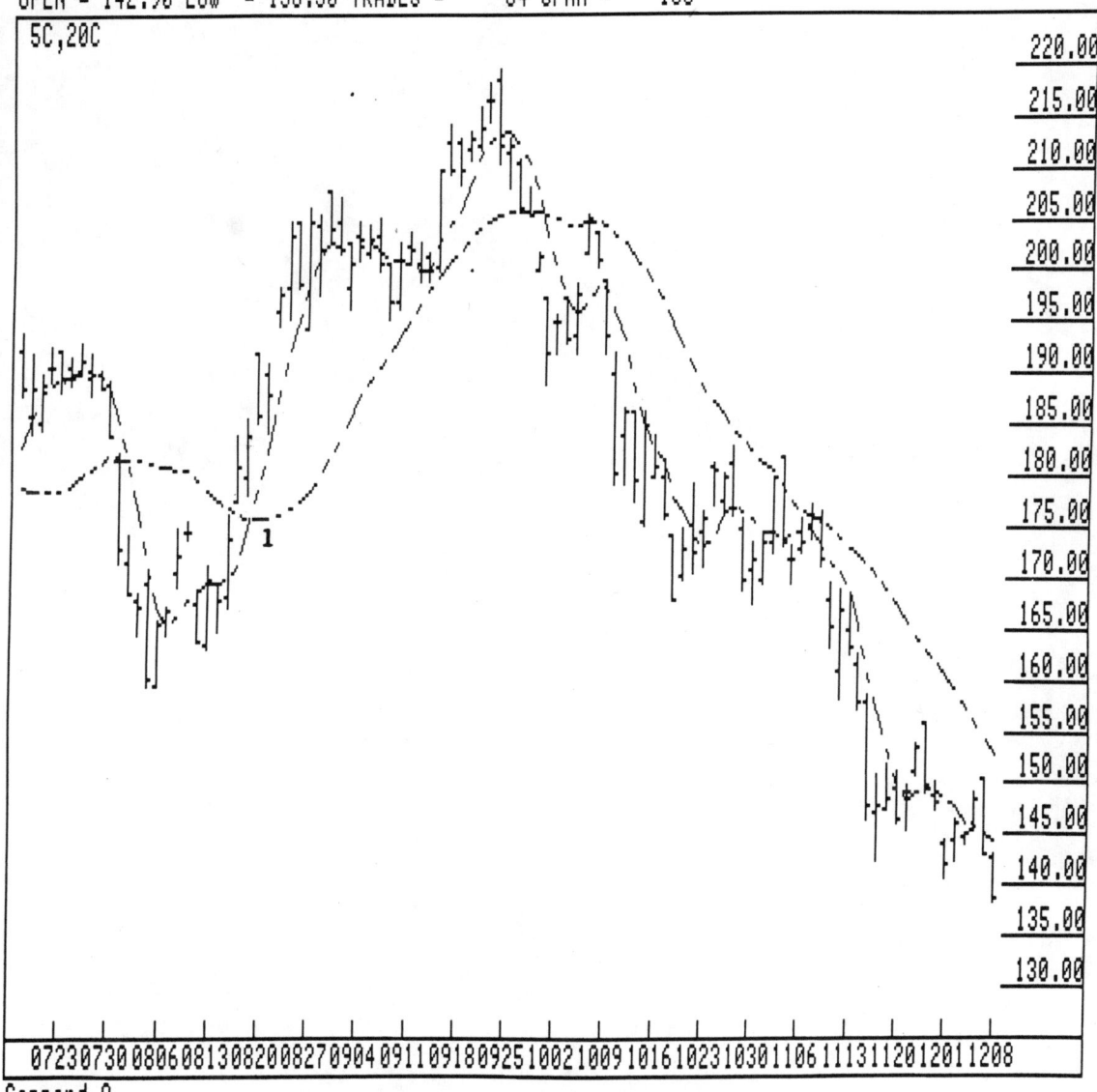

FINAL EXAMINATION

Final Examination Answer Sheet

FIGURE 1

1. The breakout at point a above the peak at point 2 initiated an <u>uptrend</u> / downtrend / neutral trend (circle one).

2. The "sell signal" at point b broke the major up trendline. The up trendline should be drawn below points <u>3</u> and <u>5</u> (fill in the blanks).

3. The selloff from points 8 to 9 shows three downside gaps. The downside gap at b is a <u>breakaway</u> / measuring / exhaustion gap?

4. The two peaks at 6 and 8 show a <u>double top</u> reversal pattern.

5. The bottom at point 9 shows a gap on either side. This type of gap pattern is called an <u>island reversal</u>.

FIGURE 2

6. During the uptrend, the downside correction from point 5 to 6 most resembles a <u>flag</u> / pennant?

7. The breakdown at point 12 appears to complete a <u>double top</u> reversal pattern.

8. Assuming the height of the topping pattern (the vertical distance between points 9 and 10) is about $25, the minimum downside target from the sell signal at $420 measures to <u>$395</u>.

9. Just prior to the first peak (at point 9), a gap shows up prominently. This is a breakaway / measuring / <u>exhaustion</u> gap.

10. After support at $400 was broken on the downside, a down trendline should have been drawn connecting which two peaks? <u>11</u> / 13 / <u>15</u> (circle two).

FIGURE 3

11. The major up trendline should be drawn below points 1 and 3.

12. The intermediate decline from point 2 to 3 is an example of a 33% / 50% / 67% retracement?

13. The sideways price pattern following the peak at 4 can best be described as a triangle.

14. That type of pattern described in the previous question is usually a reversal / continuation pattern.

15. If the trend were to turn downward, the previous peak at point 2 would now function as a support / resistance level.

FIGURE 4

16. During the initial rally, three gaps are shown at points a, b, and c. The middle gap at point b is a breakaway / measuring / exhaustion gap.

17. Of the three "gap" types, the filling of the exhaustion gap is most often a warning that a turn in the trend is near.

18. The large formation, from points 2 to 6, most resembles a symmetrical triangle.

19. In this case, that type of pattern would normally signal higher / lower prices.

20. The upside measurement from this type of pattern is usually the width / height of the pattern?

FIGURE 5

21. About halfway through the upleg 1-2, a small consolidation pattern is visible at point a. That pattern most closely resembles a pennant.

22. That type of pattern (at point a) rarely lasts more than 1 / 3 / 5 weeks in an uptrend.

23. During the subsequent decline from point 2 to 3, the price formation (b, c, d, e, f, g) resembles a symmetrical triangle.

24. Assuming the height of the previous consolidation pattern is $100, and the breakdown point (h) is at $560, the minimum downside target would be to $460.

25. A small gap appears just above the recent action (at point i). The ability of prices to move above the gap would signal higher / lower prices.

FIGURE 6

26. The chart along the bottom of this figure is the RSI line, which is used as an oscillator. At this point, the RSI line is overbought / oversold / <u>neutral</u>.

27. Two peaks in the RSI line can be seen at points a and b. That type of pattern usually warns the analyst of higher / <u>lower</u> prices in that type of situation.

28. Two troughs are seen in the RSI line at points c and d at about the same level. Given the market conditions, that type of formation is usually a sign of <u>higher</u> / lower prices.

29. At present, prices are in a neutral trading range. If prices were to break out to the upside, what would the upside target be utilizing the "measured move" technique? Answer: <u>approximately</u> <u>19.50</u>. (accept 19.00–20.00).

30. As a general rule, it is better to initiate long positions when the RSI line is an overbought / <u>oversold</u> condition.

FIGURE 7

31. The two peaks at points 1 and 2 combine to form a <u>double top</u> reversal pattern.

32. The bottom at point 3 shows a day where prices open in new low ground, then close higher on the day. These significant one-day turns are usually called <u>key reversal days.</u>

33. These days described in the previous question are considered more significant if volume for the day is <u>heavier</u> / lighter.

34. At the present time, the RSI oscillator along the bottom of the chart is overbought / oversold / <u>neutral</u>.

35. Trough b on the oscillator chart is higher than trough a. That type of market situation usually calls for <u>higher</u> / lower prices.

FIGURE 8

36. The two lines along the bottom of the chart are part of the stochastic oscillator formulation. Over the past week, the oscillator has just given a short-term "buy" / "<u>sell</u>" signal.

37. The major up trendline on such a chart should connect which two points? <u>1</u> and <u>3.</u>

38. A buying situation is usually indicated when the dotted (K line) is <u>above</u> / under the solid (D line).

39. A selling situation is usually indicated when the dotted (K line) is above / <u>under</u> the solid (D line).

40. The buy or sell signal is considered <u>stronger</u> / weaker if both lines are moving in the same direction at the time of the crossover.

FIGURE 9

41. The two curving lines are the 10- and 40-day moving averages. At this point, the two lines are in a buying / <u>selling</u> condition.

42. The crossing of the two lines at point 1 was a buy / <u>sell</u> signal.

43. The crossing of the two lines at point 2 was a <u>buy</u> / sell signal.

44. The crossing of the two lines at point 3 was a buy / <u>sell</u> signal.

45. The crossing of the two lines at point 4 was a <u>buy</u> / sell signal.

FIGURE 10

46. The two moving average lines are 5 and 20 days. Using shorter moving average lines produces <u>more</u> / fewer signals.

47. Using shorter moving average lines produces <u>faster</u> / slower signals.

48. The moving average crossing at point 1 gave a <u>buy</u> / sell signal.

49. At present, the moving average alignment is bullish / <u>bearish</u>.

50. The fact that the two lines are fairly wide apart at the moment suggests that the downtrend will probably accelerate / <u>consolidate</u>.